The REGULATORY RISK MANAGEMENT Handbook

1998–1999 Edition

PriceWaterhouseCoopers

SHARPE PROFESSIONAL
An imprint of M.E. Sharpe, INC.

Copyright © PricewaterhouseCoopers, 1999

All rights reserved. No part of this book may be reproduced in any form without written permission from the publisher, M. E. Sharpe, Inc., 80 Business Park Drive, Armonk, New York 10504

This publication is designed to provide accurate and authoritative information in regard to the subject matter covered. It is sold with the understanding that the publisher is not engaged in rendering legal, accounting, or other professional service. If legal advice or other expert assistance is required, the services of a competent professional person should be sought.

—*From the Declaration of Principles jointly adopted by a Committee of the American Bar Association and a Committee of Publishers and Associations*

ISBN 0-7656-0266-0
ISSN 1090-2554

Printed in the United States of America

(IPC) 10 9 8 7 6 5 4 3 2 1

TABLE OF CONTENTS

	Introduction	3
I.	Introduction to the U.S. Regulatory System	5
II.	Risk-Focused Examination	13
III.	Internal and External Audit	21
IV.	Organization and Duties of a Compliance Function	37
V.	Examination Management	47
VI.	Information Systems	53
VII.	The Year 2000	109
VIII.	Financial Institutions Ratings Systems	121
IX	Regulatory Enforcement	177
X.	U.S. Sentencing Guidelines	189
XI.	Interagency Safety and Soundness Guidelines	193
	Index	197

The REGULATORY RISK MANAGEMENT Handbook

Introduction

The Regulatory Handbook Series

For six years the **PricewaterhouseCoopers** Regulatory Advisory Services practice has published this series of handbooks. Our original purpose was to provide the firm and its financial institution clients with a summary of the major federal laws and regulations enforced through examinations by the federal financial regulatory agencies. In the editions we have published to date, our emphasis has been the explanation of the laws and regulations.

In 1997, we introduced *The Regulatory Risk Management Handbook* in response to the changed direction of the regulators and the financial services industry. It focuses on the process of financial institution supervision and how financial institution management can manage that process as it affects their institution's activities and operations.

Examiners place a heavy emphasis on risk management. This *Handbook* will help management adapt to this changed regulatory environment.

In the *Handbook* you will find chapters on effectively organizing a compliance function, what the examiners will expect from internal and external audit and best practices for managing an examination. These chapters will aid in managing the most direct forms of regulatory risk — criticisms in an examination report.

We have included a section on information systems examinations because of the increased importance of those examinations. Information systems affect all form of risk within an institution. Thus, management should understand and control these risks. And understanding the process of this specialized examination will be one important way to do so.

Finally, we have included some general information that will clarify the regulatory system. We have an overview of the bank regulatory system to serve as a refresher course for management, which may have concentrated on one sector of the industry. The chapter on financial institution ratings systems will be helpful in understanding an examiner's decisions and explanation of them.

The information contained in this handbook is current through February 1, 1998.

PwC Regulatory Advisory Services

The **PricewaterhouseCoopers** Regulatory Advisory Services practice in Washington, D.C., consists of former senior federal bank regulators, attorneys, and bankers who advise their clients on a broad range of U.S. bank regulatory and supervisory issues. The group is prepared to assist any financial institution in developing an effective compliance program or in evaluating its existing compliance program. Regulatory Advisory Services also is prepared to conduct reviews of an institution's policies and procedures in a particular area as well as on-site examinations to assist the institution in evaluating its level of compliance or in preparing for a regulatory exam.

If you want additional information about the material contained in this *Handbook,* or about the compliance services offered by **PricewaterhouseCoopers** Regulatory Advisory Services, please call:

Paul G. Nelson	(202) 414-4331
C. Westbrook Murphy	(202) 414-4301
Gary M. Welsh	(202) 414-4311
Paul Allan Schott	(202) 822-4272
Jeffrey P. Lavine	(202) 414-4320
David R. Sapin	(202) 414-4321
Kevin Foster	(202) 414-4335

I. Introduction to the U.S. Regulatory System

Banks and Other Financial Intermediaries 6

Bank Regulation in the United States 8

Federal and State Regulation 11

Banks and Other Financial Intermediaries

The United States has many different providers of financial services. To distinguish among them, we use the terms *bank* and *banking* to describe the segment of the U.S. financial services industry that holds special charters from the federal government or from a state government to conduct the general business of banking.

U.S. banks engage in a broad range of banking and financial activities, including, for example, trust activities and the making of mortgage and consumer loans. Historically, however, banks have emphasized accepting demand deposits (with the associated functions of clearing checks and providing a payments system) and serving the credit needs of industry, commerce, and agriculture (making commercial loans).

Commercial Banks

In these Regulatory Handbooks, we refer to institutions engaged in these historic banking functions as *commercial banks* to distinguish them from other types of U.S. deposit-taking institutions. Deposits in commercial banks are insured by the federal government through the Bank Insurance Fund (BIF) of the FDIC.

Commercial banks generally exercise a broader range of powers than other U.S. depository institutions, such as savings associations and credit unions. Commercial banks may accept demand, savings, time, and money-market deposits, and make third-party payments on checks drawn on customer accounts. In addition, the federal or state statutes controlling a commercial bank's activities allow it to engage in a variety of other specifically enumerated activities, such as:

- Discounting and negotiating promissory notes, drafts, bills of exchange, and other evidences of debt;

- Buying and selling foreign exchange, coin, and bullion;

- Acting as agent or fiduciary; and

- Buying or selling securities for the account of its customers.

State banks sometimes exercise broader powers than national banks, although federal law limits state bank activities that could pose risks to the Federal Deposit Insurance Fund.

Other Depository Institutions

In the United States, there are several other types of depository institutions that

Introduction to the U.S. Regulatory System 7

perform bank-like functions. These more specialized deposit-taking institutions include:

- Savings associations, which engage primarily in residential real estate lending and consumer lending and deposit-taking; and

- Credit unions, which principally provide a source of personal and consumer loans to individuals with a common employer, or to individuals who belong to the same organization or possess some other form of a "common bond."

Deposits in these institutions, like deposits in banks, are also insured by agencies of the federal government — the Savings Association Insurance Fund (SAIF) of the FDIC for savings associations and the National Credit Union Administration (NCUA) for credit unions.

Recently, competition and economic pressures have eroded the once clearly defined boundaries among deposit-taking institutions. Propelled by these forces, depository institutions have expanded their original credit, depository, and other nonbank financial services activities. These developments have produced significant changes in federal and state laws to permit a greater degree of homogeneity in the financial services offered by nominally different depository institutions.

> Recently, competition and economic pressure have eroded the once clearly defined bound areas among deposit-taking institutions. Propelled by these forces, depository institutions have expanded their original credit, depository, and other nonbank financial services activities.

Nondepository Financial Intermediaries

Besides the blurring of distinctions among depository institutions, explosive growth is occurring in the activities of nondepository financial services companies. These companies include securities firms, mutual funds, insurance companies, consumer finance, leasing and mortgage companies, and lending and finance subsidiaries of major industrial companies. The next wave of competition is likely to come from high technology, especially telecommunications firms capable of offering sophisticated electronic banking products in cyberspace. Many financial products or services offered by these non-depository businesses are indistinguishable from — and compete directly with — the products and services offered by depository financial institutions.

Nondepository financial services companies are largely free of the complex web of regulation that applies to banks, savings associations, and other federally insured deposit-taking institutions. Typically, such non-depository companies are not subject to the same types of examination, reserve, and capital requirements or community reinvestment obligations and geographic restrictions that affect insured deposit-taking institutions. These financial services companies thus possess some regulatory competitive advantages over insured depository institutions.

Bank Regulation in the United States

All U.S. depository institutions, including banks, are subject to a high degree of government regulation, the principal features of which include:

Licensing and Approval

Each depository institution must obtain a license or special charter from a federal or state regulatory authority. Nearly all depositories are required to have federal deposit insurance, which requires a separate application. Additional approvals or notifications to regulatory authorities are required to open deposit-taking branch offices, and are sometimes required to establish subsidiaries or to engage in new activities.

Limited Powers

A depository institution may engage only in the deposit-taking, lending, exchange, or other financial activities expressly authorized by law or regulation or in activities considered incidental or closely related to its banking business. Thus, U.S. depository institutions may not, for example, engage or invest in industrial or commercial activities such as mining, manufacturing, agriculture, and merchandising.

Supervisory Oversight

Through periodic reports and through regular on-site examinations, federal and/or state regulators closely monitor the operations of each depository institution to evaluate both its financial soundness and its compliance with applicable laws and regulations. These regulatory authorities possess extensive supervisory powers and may order the correction of any deficiencies or illegalities and may close a severely troubled or failing institution.

Deposit Insurance

Almost all U.S.-chartered depository institutions must obtain deposit insurance from the BIF, which fund insures each depositor's accounts in a U.S. bank up to a maximum of $100,000. The FDIC possesses examination and enforcement powers over all insured institutions and routinely exercises those powers at state-chartered institutions that are not members of the Federal Reserve System.

Reserve Requirements

Congress created the Federal Reserve System as an independent central bank to govern U.S. monetary policy. It is a federal system, composed basically of a central governmental agency — the Board of Governors ("Board") in Washington, D.C., and 12 regional Federal Reserve Banks. Each depository institution in the United States is subject to monetary policy reserve requirements imposed by the Board, which reserves must equal a specified percentage of the institution's domestic deposits. Reserves must be held (i) in the form of vault cash, (ii) in accounts with the Federal Reserve Banks, or (iii) in pass-through correspondent accounts with U.S. banks that are members of the Federal Reserve System or with specialized government instrumentalities (for savings associations and credit unions). Depository institutions that maintain required reserves may meet liquidity needs from time to time by borrowing funds from the Federal Reserve Banks.

Holding Companies

Federal law prohibits a company from obtaining control of a bank without prior approval of the Board. A company owning a bank — defined as a *bank holding company* — and the company's nonbank subsidiaries may not engage in any activity that is not closely related to banking or otherwise not permitted by law or regulation.

Any company owning or controlling two or more savings associations (a "savings and loan holding company") has approval and activity restrictions similar to those imposed on bank holding companies. The activities of a company owning just one savings association (a "unitary savings and loan holding company") are not so limited, thus allowing a commercial firm to own a single savings association.

Geographic Restrictions

Commercial Banks

Each state regulates the establishment of bank branches within its borders. Most states — including New York, California, and Florida — permit their banks to branch on a statewide basis. Some states — currently 10 in number — impose limits on branching within the state.

In 1994, Congress acted to permit banks to establish branches in more than one state, subject to a number of conditions. The Riegle-Neal Interstate Banking and Branching Efficiency Act of 1994 (the "Interstate Act") allows interstate branching to occur primarily through the merger of banks in different states owned by the same bank holding company. The Interstate Act permits interstate branching by merger to occur nationwide effective June 1, 1997, unless a state enacted a law *opting-out* of permitting such mergers within its borders. If a state decided to *opt-out,* banks headquartered in such state cannot acquire and merge banks outside the state. While two states — Texas and Montana — "opted-out," 48 states, as well as the District of Columbia and Puerto Rico, "opted-in" to permit such interstate branching by merger. Thirty-six of these states voted to allow interstate branching by merger before the nationwide trigger date of June 1, 1997.

The Interstate Act also permits a bank to establish in another state a *de novo* branch (i.e., a newly established branch that does not result from the merger of existing offices), but only if the host state affirmatively opts-in by enacting legislation permitting such *de novo* branches of banks headquartered in other states. Fifteen states enacted such *de novo* legislation; however, with few exceptions, states only allow such *de novo* branching on a reciprocal basis with other states.

Bank Holding Companies

Effective September 21, 1995, bank holding companies may acquire bank subsidiaries in any state, despite any state laws. Earlier restrictions on interstate bank acquisitions had been largely removed through state action. The Interstate Act eliminated all remaining state restrictions on such acquisitions.

The Interstate Act also allows bank subsidiaries of a bank holding company to establish certain agency arrangements among themselves that allow them to function more like a branch system. For example, a bank affiliate in one state could receive payments on loans made by a bank affiliate in another state.

Nonbank financial subsidiaries of a bank holding company, such as mortgage companies, securities brokerage firms, consumer finance companies, factoring companies, and trust companies, are not subject to interstate banking restrictions and may operate nationwide.

Savings Associations

Savings associations have traditionally been less restricted geographically than banks both on an in-state and interstate basis. Federal savings associations are not subject to any federal interstate branching restrictions. state statutes also sometimes permit savings associations to establish branch offices in more than one state, subject to prior approval by the supervisory agency.

Securities Activities

Since 1933, the Glass-Steagall Act has limited the involvement of depository institutions or their affiliates in buying, selling, underwriting, or dealing in corporate debt and equity securities. Because of decisions by the courts and federal regulatory agencies, these limitations have been rapidly eroding.

Bank holding company securities affiliates of commercial banks may underwrite and sell the commercial paper, debt instruments, and other securities of their corporate customers (so-called ineligible securities subject to certain overall limitations on the scope of such business). At present, revenues from such ineligible activities may not exceed 25 percent of a bank holding company securities affiliate's gross revenues.

Federal and State Regulation

The choice of a federal or state license has created a parallel, or *dual,* system of bank licensing and regulation in the United States. There are more than 9,000 commercial banks in the United States, of which approximately one-third are chartered and primarily supervised by the federal government. These banks are called national banks. The various state governments have chartered and supervise the remaining commercial banks. While there are more state banks than national banks, national banks have a greater percentage of total bank assets in the United States.

Three federal agencies currently have regulatory authority over commercial banks. The OCC, a bureau of the Treasury Department, charters, regulates, examines, and supervises national banks. The FDIC insures bank deposits and is the federal regulator, supervisor, and examining agency for state-chartered banks that are not members of the Federal Reserve System.

The Board is the nation's central bank and regulates bank reserves, provides discount window liquidity and lender of last resort facilities to U.S. banking institutions, and operates and regulates much of the payments system. The Board also serves as the federal supervisor, regulator, and examining agency for state-chartered banks that are members of the Federal Reserve System. The Board also has regulatory authority over bank holding companies, Edge Act and Agreement (International Banking) Corporations, and the international operations of national and state member banks.

State and federal regulation of commercial banks often overlaps. State-chartered banks, for example, are subject (i) to regulation by a state regulatory authority; (ii) to federal regulation by the FDIC, which insures their deposits; and (iii) to federal regulation by the Board, which establishes and administers reserve requirements and regulates all bank holding companies. Federally chartered national banks are governed by federal banking laws, but also are regulated by state laws in certain areas, such as branching, the exercise of fiduciary powers, and transactional and contractual relationships.

While a number of proposals have been put forward to consolidate the domestic bank regulatory, supervisory, and examination functions of the three federal banking agencies, there has been little political or industry consensus on how such consolidation should occur.

> Regulatory structures are changing. On January 1, 1999, the separate deposit insurance funds for banks and thrift institutions will merge into a single deposit insurance fund.

II. Risk-Focused Examination System

Renewed Emphasis by Regulators 14

Agency Differences in Risk-Focused Examinations 14

OCC and FRB Examination Process 16

FDIC Risk Focus 16

Office of Thrift Supervision Risk Focus 17

Effect on Audit and Compliance Activities 18

Risk Management Advice 19

Renewed Emphasis by Regulators

The risk-focused examination (or supervision by risk) is a newly popular topic in financial institution regulation. It is not a new concept, however, for the techniques go back 20 years or more to the time when the agencies began to emphasize the top-down approach to bank examination.

In the past several years, the bank regulators have revised and enhanced the top-down method to evolve the risk-focused supervisory approach to evaluating financial institutions. Several stimuli caused the movement to risk-focused examinations. Congress, in FDICIA, asked the agencies to develop a system to measure the impact of interest rate risk on each financial institution's capital. After years of working on the problem, the agencies have been unable to develop a simple calculation to impose as a rule for all financial institutions. But the emphasis on this sort of risk spurred development of interest rate risk monitoring systems.

The evolutionary process accelerated with the regulators' recognition of the inability of existing examination procedures to address problems in derivatives portfolios. The speed with which derivative products change made the periodic on-site examination an inadequate protection against possibly systemic losses. To respond to the risks derivatives pose, the regulators had to develop off-site means of anticipating problems.

A further cause of the shift to risk focus may also be the perception of regulatory burden. The complexity of examinations has grown with new regulatory requirements and with industry consolidation. On-site examinations now take longer and use more examining staff than in the past. To reduce interruptions to institutions' business and to reduce their own administrative costs, the agencies have shifted to the risk-focused examination. The change allows the agencies to do more of the work off-site and at a lower cost.

Agency Differences in Risk-Focused Examinations

As shown in the table below, the Office of the Comptroller of the Currency and the Federal Reserve System have identified nine and six risk categories, respectively. Despite the difference in the number of categories, the risks covered are nearly identical.

The Federal Reserve includes the OCC's concepts of interest rate risk and foreign exchange risk in its market risk definition. The OCC's strategic risk concept is part of the Fed's legal or operational risk.

Comptroller of the Currency	Federal Reserve
Credit Risk – The risk of an obligor's failure to perform as agreed. An obligor includes a counterparty or issuer as well as a borrower.	Credit Risk – The risk that an obligor or counterparty will fail to perform an obligation.
Interest Rate Risk – The risk arising from movements in interest rates. It includes matters of repricing, basis, yield curves, and options. It also includes interest-related hedging and pricing.	
Liquidity Risk – The risk arising from the bank's inability to meet obligations. Liquidity risk includes the inability to manage unplanned decreases or changes in funding sources, and the inability to recognize or address changes in market conditions affecting the ability to liquidate assets quickly with minimal loss in value.	Liquidity Risk – The potential that an institution will be unable to meet its obligations because of an inability to liquidate assets, or obtain adequate funding, or unwind or offset certain exposures because of inadequate market depth or market disruptions.
Price Risk – The risk from changing values of portfolios. It arises from market making, dealing, and position taking activities for interest rate, foreign exchange, equity, and commodity markets.	Market Risk – The risk to a financial institution's condition resulting from adverse movements in market rates or prices, such as interest rates, foreign exchange rates, or equity prices.
Foreign Exchange Risk – The risk arising from movement of foreign exchange rates. Also known as transfer risk, it affects cross-border investing and operations.	
Transaction Risk – The risk from problems with service of product delivery. Also known as operating risk, it arises from internal controls, information systems, employee integrity, and operating processes.	Operational Risk – The risk from the potential that inadequate information systems, operational problems, breaches in internal controls fraud, or unforeseen catastrophes will result in unexpected losses.
Compliance Risk – The risk arising from violations or nonconformance with laws, rules, regulations, prescribed practices, or ethical standards. It includes the risk of exposure to litigation from all aspects of banking.	Legal Risk – The potential that unenforceable contracts, lawsuits, or adverse judgments can disrupt or otherwise negatively affect the operations or condition of a financial institution.
Strategic Risk – The risk from adverse business decisions or improper implementation of those decisions. This risk measures how plans systems and implementation affect a bank's franchise value.	
Reputation Risk – The risk from negative public opinion and its effect on the bank's ability to establish new relationships or service or continue preexisting relationships.	Reputational Risk – The potential that negative publicity regarding an institution's business practices, whether true or not, will cause a decline in the customer base, costly litigation, or revenue reductions.

OCC and FRB Examination Process

The examination process begins at the planning stage when agency staff make a preliminary assessment for each risk category. This internal assessment, based on previous examination findings, internal and external financial and management reports, and interviews with senior bank management, drives the examination scope. Both agencies instruct their examiners to develop risk profiles for the banks they examine. Using the risk profile, examiners will focus on where the risks are in a bank. A bank's CAMELS rating reflects the examiners' assessment of the quality of its risk management.

For both the OCC and FRB, the examination process retains its top-down character. The examiners supplement their top-down review with transactional testing, as appropriate in their judgment. Examination procedures do not incorporate new guidance on the level and degree of transactional testing suggested or required.

We expect transactional testing will be reduced and, in some cases, significantly curtailed where the examiners have concluded that sound risk management processes exist, given the level of risk perceived in the activity. We expect to see a reduction in transactional testing in two areas — compliance and lending activities. These areas traditionally use the greatest level of examiner resources given the previous high level of transactional testing. These areas, thus, offer the greatest opportunity to create a more efficient examination process and, to reduce the regulatory burden.

FDIC Risk Focus

The FDIC has also developed a risk focus to its examinations. Unlike the OCC and FRB it has not developed a catalog of named risks to which an institution may be exposed. Likewise, the FDIC's examinations are more transaction-focused and less risk-focused than those of the OCC and FRB. The FDIC has, instead, worked to develop a system that former FDIC Chairman Helfer describes as bridging "the gap that separates the macro from the micro perspective." When the FDIC completes its process, it will analyze risk in an institution along product or functional lines.

Under the FDIC's method, the agency will use statistical and economic analysis as a factor in bank examinations. The analysis is an attempt to give examiners a structured and consistent means of identifying the levels and trends of risk. The FDIC intends the data to allow an examiner to review each bank's condition.

To assist the examiners, the FDIC is developing flowcharts for some of the risks a bank may face in a function or a product. The flowcharts specify the degree of detail an examiner should give to any particular risk.

The FDIC has its flowchart completed on interest rate risk and has begun testing it in some regions. The agency initially will develop flowcharts for loans, investment securities, funds management, capital, earnings, and interest rate risk.

The FDIC's development of these flowcharts has been slower than anticipated. However, the agency intends to have as many as 20 of these flowcharts to diagnose risks in all aspects of a financial institution's activities. For instance, within the lending area, examiners would use separate flowcharts for commercial loans and for consumer loans, rather than one general lending flowchart for both forms of loans.

Office of Thrift Supervision Risk Focus

Unlike the other three regulators, the OTS has not publicized a shift in its examination methods. OTS officials do assert, however, that the agency has had risk-focused examinations since 1989, when it succeeded to the responsibilities of the old Federal Home Loan Bank Board.

In the view of the OTS, the other three agencies' change to a risk-focused examination means that they will be doing more analytical work off-site.

The OTS methods already required this off-site work and, thus, the agency considers itself as anticipating the others' moves to a risk-focused system.

The OTS-supervised institutions characteristically have depended on long-term mortgage lending rather than shorter-term consumer or commercial lending. As a result, those institutions have a greater interest rate risk than commercial or consumer lenders and the OTS has had to develop sophisticated interest-risk analytical tools to assist in its supervision.

Institutions regulated by the OTS are subject to all other risks affecting financial institutions. Using definitions paralleling the OCC and FRB definitions, the OTS monitors thrift institutions for these other categories of risk:

- Credit risk – the risk that borrowers, counterparties, or issuers of securities will not repay their obligations as contractually agreed;

- Operational risk – the risk flowing from inadequate system information, breaches in internal controls, inconsistent application of an institution's policies or procedures, or operational problems;

- Market risk – the risk resulting from changes in interest rates, exchange rates, or commodity prices. In a thrift, market risk is virtually identical to interest rate risk;

- Liquidity risk – the risk that the institution does not maintain liquid assets or sufficient ready access to funds to meet its obligations in a timely manner;

- Legal and compliance risk – the possibility that contracts, lawsuits, or adverse judgments may negatively affect operations, capital, or profits; and

- Strategic risk – the risk of loss from business decisions or investments that the board or management do not adequately evaluate or control.

Effect on Audit and Compliance Activities

The risk focused approach and expected reduction in testing will be influenced by an increased review by the examiners of the audit activities of the institution. Increased reliance on the activities and work of audits, both, internal and external, is consistent with the new approach in determining both examination scope and evaluating the internal control structure.

The Federal Reserve's Division of Banking Supervision and Regulation, in its May 24, 1996, communication to each of the Federal Reserve Banks ("Risk Focused Safety and Soundness Examinations and Inspections" SR 96-14 SUP) stated:

> Examiners should meet with internal auditors or other personnel responsible for evaluating internal controls and review internal control risk assessments, work plans, reports, workpapers, and related communication with the audit committee or board of directors.

With respect to external auditors, the memorandum stated:

> Depending on the size and complexity of the activities conducted by the institution, the examiner should also consider conducting a similar review of the work performed by the institution's external auditors. Such a review often provides added insight into key areas by detailing the nature and testing of those areas that have been conducted by auditors in their course of their work.

In the past, examiners reviewed external audit programs, workpapers, and testing infrequently and on an exception basis. However, as the regulatory agencies explore new examination techniques to enhance supervision, they are recognizing the potential for broader cooperation and coordination with internal and external auditors.

The new examination approach is keyed to an assessment of each of the identified risk categories. Examiners will assess these risks across product, business, and legal entity lines resulting in a consolidated conclusion by the examiners as to the level and management of those risks by category.

There are several important aspects to this assessment process. The examiners will expect to see a documented and fairly consistent approach by management to control, measure, monitor, and report on risk across the organization. In the area of credit, for example, a financial institution should expect examiners to apply the same risk management approach and credit analysis to nontraditional credit exposures as they have to loans and leases. The nontraditional sources of credit exposure include:

- Trading activities;
- Investments;
- Placements;
- Capital market instruments; and
- Payments and settlements.

This risk-focused method will also drive a broader review of institutional activities including those that examiners previously have subjected to limited scrutiny. As a result, we expect the agencies to shift examination resources to several new areas or activities where the perceived risks are growing. Examples of these include:

- Off-balance sheet credit exposures;
- Agency transactions;
- Advisory services; and
- Transaction processing.

Risk Management Advice

As a means to enhance an institution's understanding of regulatory concerns, priorities, and activities, we make these suggestions. Through external and internal audit and through the compliance staff, a financial institution should:

- Maintain a dialogue with senior examination staff. Meetings prior to the start of the examination and at the conclusion are helpful to become aware of examination scope, reliance on audit activities, and significant findings.

- Consider the level of transactional testing within the institution that external auditors, internal audit, or other "testers" provide. Make certain that management has determined which areas of the institution's activities are critical and that these areas are subject to testing. An examiner may curtail testing if others are conducting effective testing for the institution.

- Ensure that the audit plans, programs, workpapers, and reports reflect a thorough and thoughtful approach to risk assessment of the financial institution's businesses.

- Review the scope of its external audit to ensure that it is responsive to emerging or nontraditional credit risks.

III. Internal and External Audit

Introduction 22

Risk-Based Auditing 22

Internal Auditing Function 25

External Auditing Function 31

References 35

Introduction

Sound audit functions are vital to helping an institution's board of directors and management monitor and control risks that affect the institution. The board of directors and management are responsible for an institution's operations, financial reporting, and compliance. Although audit functions may encompass oversight or consideration of many different risks, they are likely to focus more on the implications of transaction and compliance risk.

This section covers the purpose, organization, management, and scope of an internal audit function and the same, although more generally, for external audit. It also discusses risk-based auditing and outsourcing of internal audit. For coverage of statutory audit requirements, see the Audits and Accounting Standards section of *The Commercial Banking Regulatory Handbook*.

Risk-Based Auditing

Financial institutions and examiners are focusing more attention on identifying, controlling, and managing risk and its effect on how institutions are managed and supervised.

Risk-based auditing is used to increase auditing efficiency and effectiveness and to control costs. It focuses on controlling and maintaining risks at an acceptable level and monitoring management and staff performance. The basic objectives of risk-based auditing are similar to any other auditing objectives:

- Risk identification and classification;
- Internal control system evaluation;
- Integrity of records;
- Adequacy of policies, procedures, practices, and standards;
- Compliance with laws and regulations;
- Qualifications of personnel; and
- Corrective actions on identified deficiencies.

Risk assessment models help in allocating auditing resources to the areas of greatest risk. Major risk factors include:

- Nature of the transactions (e.g., dollar and transaction volume);

- Nature of the operating environment (e.g., changes in volume growth);

- Internal controls and security (e.g., adequacy of control policies and procedures);

- Human resources (e.g., experience of management, staff, turnover); and

- Senior management oversight.

Auditors should assess these risk factors to help establish audit scope and frequency by assigning risk levels (e.g., high, medium, low) to each risk factor and then weighting the elements within each factor to get an overall risk-weighted score. In addition to the score from a risk assessment model, the audit management and staff should use their own judgment by evaluating other qualitative factors in setting audit frequency. Audits performed using a risk-based approach normally should not exceed a four-year cycle for low-risk areas. High-risk and medium-risk areas should generally be audited within 12 to 24 months, respectively, at a maximum.

Transaction Risk

Transaction risk is the risk to earnings or capital arising from problems with service or product delivery. This risk is a function of internal controls, information systems, employee integrity, and operating processes. Transaction risk exists in all products and services. Exposure to loss can result from failure to process or produce items in an accurate, thorough, and timely manner. The audit should assess the adequacy of controls and information systems, the adequacy of employees, the accuracy and integrity of systems, and the contingency backup for crises and external events.

Compliance Risk

Compliance risk is the risk to earnings or capital arising from violations of or nonconformance with laws, rules, regulations, prescribed practices, or ethical standards. The risk also arises in situations where the laws or rules governing certain bank products or activities, or the activities of the institution's clients, may be ambiguous or untested. Compliance risk exposes the institution to fines, civil money penalties, payment of damages, and voiding of contracts. Compliance risk can lead to diminished reputation, reduced franchise value, more limited business opportunities, lessened expansion potential, and lack of contract enforceability. An institution's internal auditing function should do a broad assessment of transaction and compliance risk. An independent public accountant should focus more on the risk aspect of material misstatements in financial statements, compliance with certain provisions of the Federal Deposit Insurance Corporation Improvement Act (FDICIA), and adherence to generally accepted accounting principles.

Policies and Procedures

Institutions should have policies and procedures for their risk-based auditing system. The policies and procedures should be approved by an audit committee and the board of directors and reviewed and reaffirmed annually by the board of directors.

Written Standards

All risk-based auditing systems should have written standards to ensure consistent application of factors, weights, and overall scores. An institution should have sufficient documentation to support any assigned weights. Written standards should define:

- The ranges of scores or assessments that are low, medium, and high risk;

- The audit cycle frequency for each area based on the scores or assessments;

- Minimum audit intervals (e.g., every unit must be audited at least every four years);

- Cases where a scoring system may not work and auditor judgment should take over; and

- Minimum documentation requirements to support assessment decisions.

Standards should also address time frames for assessing each department. Auditing management and staff should periodically evaluate risk in each department or function. A recommended time frame would be at least yearly, but the standards should define key indicators for evaluating a department or function more often. Both line department managers and auditors should perform the risk evaluation in all departments and functions. Line managers should review risk assessments for reasonableness and provide feedback. Auditors should periodically review the results of internal control processes and analyze financial or operational data for any effect on a risk weighting. Institution management has an obligation to keep auditors current on all major changes in departments or functions, such as the introduction of a new product, implementation of a new system, changes in organization or staff, or other changes.

Proper training of auditors in risk assessment is essential. Auditors should have a strong knowledge of business functions to adequately determine and review key indicators.

Internal Auditing Function

Audit Charter

The institution's board of directors should adopt a charter or issue a policy statement establishing clearly the responsibilities of internal auditors. The charter should identify the purpose, responsibilities, and authority of the audit department. It should state clearly the auditor's right to access all records, policies, plans, procedures, and properties and to question personnel relevant to the matters under review. The audit charter should include a statement of audit independence and support from the board of directors.

An internal audit evaluates the day-to-day controls to ascertain whether activities are conducted in compliance with acceptable accounting methods and standards set forth by the board of directors and senior management. The internal auditor is properly concerned with all phases of business activity and, therefore, must look beyond accounting and financial records to obtain a full understanding of the operations under review. Auditors should furnish management with analyses, appraisals, recommendations, and other comments concerning activities reviewed. These comments will assist management in using its resources more effectively.

An institution should have an internal auditing function that is appropriate to the institution's size and the nature and scope of its activities. An internal audit function should provide for:

- Auditing that is independent and objective;

- Staffing by persons qualified to perform the audit;

- Monitoring, testing, and reviewing of internal controls and information systems;

- Documentation of tests, findings, and any corrective actions;

- Verification and review of management's actions to address material weaknesses; and

- Review by the institution's audit committee or board of directors of the effectiveness of the internal auditing systems.

Independence of Internal Auditors

The ability of the internal audit function to achieve its audit objectives depends, in large part, on the independence maintained by audit personnel. Frequently, internal audit's independence can be determined by its reporting lines within the organization and to whom or to what level internal audit reports results. As stated above, the internal audit function should be under the direction of the board of directors or a committee of the board.

The auditor's responsibilities should be addressed in a written position description and the auditor's reporting lines should be delineated in personnel policies. Minutes of the meetings of the audit committee and board of directors should document audit results. Internal auditors generally should not have responsibility for the accounting system, other aspects of the institution's accounting function, or any operational function not subject to independent review.

Planning the Audit

The effectiveness of any internal audit program depends on the soundness of audit practices and proper planning. The more precise the audit objectives, the more likely supporting procedures will be appropriate and carried out effectively. In general, the planning function includes:

- Setting objectives, formulating procedures, and preparing a budget;

- Obtaining sufficient resources for accomplishing the institution's audit objectives;

- Compiling a list of reports, information, and other aids to be requested from the audited area;

- Assigning responsibilities to accomplish the objectives within budget restrictions; and

- Reappraising objectives, procedures, and budgets to meet changing conditions.

> The effectiveness of any internal audit program depends on the soundness of audit practices and proper planning.

Scope and Frequency of Audit Coverage

The board, or its audit committee, should approve the internal audit schedule each year. If the auditors cannot complete the audit within the expected cycle, they should document the reasons and report them to the board or audit committee. The audit committee or the board should approve major adjustments to the schedule. The scope of the procedures and frequency of internal auditing must be sufficient to accomplish the audit objectives.

Audit Work Program

Developing the audit work program is an integral part of planning the audit. Audit work programs serve as the primary guide to the audit procedures. Each program should provide a clear, concise description of the work required, and individual procedures should be presented in a logical manner. The detailed procedures included in the program vary depending on the size and complexity of the institution's operations and the area subject to audit. In addition, an individual audit work program may encompass several departments of the institution, a single department, or specific operations within a department.

A comprehensive internal audit program should include the following elements:

1. A determination that the records of the institution are complete and adequate and that transactions are promptly and properly recorded in the accounts;

2. An accounting for the receipt of income and review of expenses to determine that they are authorized, correct in amount, and consistent with the institution's policy;

3. A check for compliance with applicable statutes and regulations;

4. A review for compliance with policies established by management or the board of directors, including verification that loans and securities have been properly approved;

5. A direct verification on a periodic basis of loan and deposit balances;

6. A determination that assets are adequately safeguarded and properly presented in financial reports, and that liabilities are completely disclosed and accounted for;

7. An assurance that collateral and other nonledger items are properly recorded and protected by effective custodial controls;

8. A validation of the authority granted to members of the organization (to make loans or sign official checks, bank drafts, internal entries, letters of authorization, deeds, transfers, and any other types of legal or accounting documents) to be certain there are no departures from established policy;

9. A review of loan losses, operating charge-offs, and the control exercised over recoveries;

10. An evaluation of the adequacy of fidelity and casualty insurance in force;

11. The preparation of a proper and complete set of working papers covering each audit;

12. The utilization of accepted verification and confirmation techniques;

13. The establishment and maintenance of an operating manual describing the specific procedures and techniques to be used by the auditor or auditing staff in performing the audit function;

14. If the institution's records are processed by an EDP servicer, a review of data controls;

15. An appraisal of the performance of personnel in accomplishing assigned internal control functions and responsibilities; and

16. Surprise examinations, where appropriate.

Organizing the Audit

Once the auditor develops the audit plan, the auditor must organize staff to accomplish it. Organizing the audit plan includes establishing a structure and a system designed to:

- Achieve the objectives;

- Assign responsibilities for carrying out the plan;

- Maintain continuity of organization and responsibility; and

- Reappraise the structure and system periodically to ensure their continued effectiveness.

Supervising the Audit

Supervision is directing, coordinating, and regulating the audit pursuant to planning requirements to assure that the audit achieves the stated objectives. The degree of supervision required depends on the competence of the auditors and sophistication and risk associated with the particular area being audited. Supervision generally includes:

- Determining the scope and frequency of audits;

- Establishing standards, including costs and quality of work, for the audit department;

- Ensuring compliance with audit standards by reviewing and signing off on completed workpapers and audit reports;

- Maintaining the audit standards by monitoring procedures, obtaining feedback, and making appropriate adjustments to meet changing conditions;

Internal and External Audit System

- Training personnel to comply with the standards; and

- Following up to ensure that management promptly responds to the audit report and that the response addresses all points as required under the audit program.

Documenting and Reporting Audit Work

The audit department should establish standards for audit workpapers and communicating findings to management. Audit workpapers should contain sufficient evidence of the tasks performed and conclusions reached. The audit work programs should contain specific steps that should lead internal auditors to a conclusion that satisfies corresponding audit objectives. Conclusions must be appropriate for the audit work performed and consistent with documented findings.

Internal auditors should communicate their findings by providing management with a written report. The report should help management to evaluate the quality of the departments audited and suggest methods for correcting or improving any adverse conditions found. Audit reports should be timely, summarize facts, and indicate the status of previously reported exceptions. The reports should contain information that is accurate and constructed and presented clearly and logically so that any negative audit report finding can more easily trigger a management decision.

Audit Follow-up

Prompt and effective management response to internal auditors' recommendations should be required as part of an audit follow-up. The audit procedures should identify clearly the methods for follow-up.

These procedures may include:

- Requesting a written management response to the audit report that identifies corrective action for each deficiency;

- Subsequent audit tests to verify resolution of deficiencies; and

- Reports to the board of directors or the audit committee concerning specific action taken or lack thereof.

When auditors note a critical deficiency, they should schedule a follow-up review to ensure that the corrective action has reduced the exposure to an acceptable level. As part of the follow-up review, auditors should document recommendations that management did not accept and the deficiencies remaining and report these results to the board.

Without follow-up, even a comprehensive internal audit program will be less effective. In many cases, the internal audit manager is responsible for monitoring the progress of audit recommendations. Monitoring techniques must be effective, yet should not impair the audit manager's relationship with operating management. For this reason, and to promote line management ownership of identified problems, an institution may prefer to appoint a senior officer to be responsible for audit follow-up.

Coordination with External Audit

Internal auditors should coordinate with external auditing efforts to ensure adequate auditing coverage and minimize duplicative efforts. Coordination of auditing efforts involves:

- Periodic meetings to discuss matters of mutual interest;

- Access to each other's auditing programs and working papers;

- Discussion and comparison of respective risk assessments;

- Exchange of audit reports and management letters; and

- Common understanding of auditing techniques, methods, and terminology.

Internal Audit Outsourcing

Institutions are increasingly evaluating the use of public accounting firms to provide traditional internal auditing services. Internal audit outsourcing takes many forms, ranging from performing limited procedures in a specific location or functional area to providing the substantial portion of an institution's entire internal auditing function. Institutions most often use audit outsourcing in specialized areas such as information systems, trust, mortgage banking, and capital markets.

> On December 22, 1997, the Federal Reserve Board and the federal banking regulators issued a policy statement on Internal Auditing Outsourcing Arrangements. The statement is designed to assure that management remains responsible for internal audit; that examiners will have full access to information; and that accountants will remain independent.

On December 22, 1997, the Federal Reserve Board and the other federal banking regulators issued a policy statement on Internal Auditing Outsourcing Arrangements. The statement is designed to assure that management remains responsible for internal audit; that examiners will have full access to information; and that accountants will remain independent. The policy statement generally provides, among other things, that:

Internal and External Audit System 31

- Directors and senior management remain responsible for periodic assessment of internal control, generally through an internal audit function;

- In outsourcing arrangements, institutions should still have adequate senior internal audit management to direct the outsourcing engagement and make the decisions required by management;

- Outsourcing arrangements may not in any way limit the access of regulators or management to audit findings and evidence such as to hinder effective supervision or prudent monitoring and risk management; and

- Independent accountants should be careful to ensure that in such arrangements they remain independent under professional standards and not assume a management or employee role in fact or appearance.

External Auditing Function

Independent audits enhance the probability that financial statements and reports to a financial institution's regulator and other users of financial statements will be accurate. The independent audit process also subjects the internal controls and the accounting policies, procedures, and records of a financial institution to periodic review.

Board of Directors' Responsibilities

The board of directors and senior management should clearly define the responsibilities of external auditors. The board may require auditors to submit engagement letters to the board before the audit begins. The letters usually discuss the scope of the audit, its length, and resulting reports. The letters may also contain summaries of essential features of the audit with schedules describing specific procedures for each area audited. They may also include biographical information on personnel involved, as well as provisions for disclosure and review of audit workpapers by the financial institution, its representatives, or regulatory examiners. In addition, the letter may specify any auditing procedures to be omitted, such as confirmation of loans or deposits, and whether the auditor is expected to render an opinion on the institution's financial statements.

When auditing an institution's financial statements, external auditors may review internal control procedures as part of their overall evaluation of internal accounting controls. The purpose of this review in a traditional financial statement audit is to understand the controls to determine the extent and nature of the substantive tests to be performed. For a full discussion of statutory audit requirements, see the Audits and Accounting Standards section of *The Commercial Banking Regulatory Handbook.*

External auditors and consultants may also provide services in the areas of auditing and special studies in addition to the financial statement audit. These additional services may include advice on the preparation of call reports and in-depth reviews of the operations of specific departments. After completing such reviews, the auditors may recommend that the institution, among other things, strengthen controls or increase efficiency, or both.

The board of directors or audit committee should analyze the adequacy of their external audit coverage. As with an internal audit, competence and independence of the auditors and the adequacy of the audit program are the major factors the board or committee should consider. If not statutorily mandated and the board or committee determines that an external audit is not necessary, it should include reasons supporting the decision in the board or committee minutes. Otherwise, the minutes should include a discussion of the engagement terms for external auditors and the scope of the audit to be performed.

Standards of Conduct

The Code of Professional Ethics for CPAs who are members of the American Institute of Certified Public Accountants (AICPA) requires that audits be performed according to generally accepted auditing standards (GAAS). GAAS, as distinct from generally accepted accounting principles, or GAAP, is concerned with the auditor's professional qualifications, the judgment the auditor exercises in performing an audit, and the quality of the audit procedures.

On the other hand, GAAP represents all the conventions, rules, and procedures that are necessary to define accepted accounting practices at a particular time. GAAP includes broad guidelines of general application and detailed practices and procedures that have been issued by the Financial Accounting Standards Board (FASB), the AICPA, the SEC, or other authoritative bodies that set accounting standards. Thus, GAAP provides guidance on financial reporting matters.

Generally Accepted Auditing Standards

GAAS is grouped into three categories: general standards, standards of fieldwork, and standards of reporting.

The general standards require that the person or persons performing the audit have adequate technical training and proficiency, that auditors maintain independence in mental attitude, and that auditors exercise due professional care in performing the audit and preparing the report.

Standards of fieldwork require that the auditors adequately plan the work; that assistants, if any, be properly supervised; that auditors study and evaluate existing internal controls to determine the audit scope and the audit procedures to be performed during the audit; and that auditors obtain sufficient evidence to formulate an opinion regarding the financial statements under audit.

Standards of reporting require that the CPA state whether the financial statements are presented in accordance with GAAP. The application of GAAP in audited financial statements and reports must achieve the fundamental objectives of financial accounting, which is to provide reliable financial information about the economic resources and obligations of a business enterprise. In addition, the informative disclosures in the financial statements must follow GAAP, or the CPA must state otherwise in the report.

GAAP recognizes that management — not the CPA — has primary responsibility for preparing the financial statements and the accompanying presentations. The auditor's responsibility is to express an opinion on the financial statements. GAAS (or the audit requirements previously set forth) requires that audits cover the following financial statements: balance sheet, income statement, statement of changes in stockholders' equity, and statement of cash flows and related footnote disclosures.

GAAS requires that CPAs plan and perform auditing procedures to obtain reasonable assurance that financial statements are free from material misstatement. Under GAAS, an audit includes examining on a test basis and should include evidence supporting the amounts and disclosures in the financial statements. An audit also includes assessing the accounting principles used and significant estimates made by management, as well as evaluating the overall financial statement presentation.

Independence

In performing their work, CPAs must be independent of those they serve. Traditionally, independence has been defined as the ability to act with integrity and objectivity. When a CPA expresses an opinion on financial statements, the CPA must maintain integrity and objectivity both in fact and appearance. The profession has adopted rules to prohibit a CPA from expressing such an opinion when the CPA has relationships that might pose a significant threat to integrity and objectivity. These relationships fall into two general categories: (a) certain financial relationships with clients, and (b) relationships in which the CPA is virtually part of management or an employee under management's control.

In accordance with the rule on independence included in the Code of Professional Ethics and related AICPA interpretations, a CPA's independence is considered impaired if, for example, during the period of his or her professional engagement, the CPA or his or her firm had any direct or material indirect financial interest in the enterprise or had any loan to or from the enterprise or any officer, director, or principal stockholder thereof. The Code of Professional Ethics permits certain exceptions to the prohibition. These include, among others, secured loans and home mortgages made according to the institution's usual terms and procedures.

External Audit Reports

The external auditor generates various types of reports and other documents, which typically include:

- The standard audit report — generally a one-page document.

- A "management letter" in which the auditor presents confidentially detailed findings and recommendations to management.

- In some cases, reports from the auditor to regulators during the audit period.

The major types of standard audit reports will never have a heading or other statement in the report that identifies which type it is. Rather, certain terminology used in the text identifies the type of report. The major types of standard audit reports are:

The unqualified report — sometimes referred to as a "clean opinion." This report states the financial statements are "presented fairly" in conformity with GAAP and that the necessary audit work was done. In addition, the auditor may add an explanation of certain circumstances that must be explained but do not affect the overall unqualified opinion.

The qualified report — which may generally have the same language as the unqualified report but will use the phrase "except for" or "with the exception of" to indicate that some problem exists. The types of problems include a lack of sufficient evidential matter, restrictions on the scope of audit work that do not require a disclaimer of opinion, or departures from GAAP in the financial statements that do not require an adverse opinion.

An adverse report — which basically concludes that, based on an audit completed in accordance with GAAS, the financial statements are not presented fairly in conformity with GAAP. Auditors rarely issue this type of report because auditors and management usually work out their differences in advance.

A disclaimer—which expresses no opinion on the financial statements. CPAs may issue a disclaimer when there has been a limitation on the scope of the audit. Scope limitations may result from inadequate accounting records of the auditee or because insufficient evidential matter existed for the auditor to be satisfied that the statements were fairly stated.

References

Audit and Accounting Guide, AICPA.

Commercial Bank Examination Manual, Federal Reserve.

DOS Manual of Examination Policies, Federal Deposit Insurance Corporation.

Internal and External Audits, Comptroller's Handbook.

Standards for the Professional Practice of Internal Auditing, Institute of Internal Auditors.

IV. Organization and Duties of a Compliance Function

General	38
Compliance Officer	38
Compliance Committee	38
Support for Senior Management	38
Support for Operating Management	39
Senior Management Responsibility	39
Oversight of Operational Management's Compliance Activities	40
Primary Responsibility for Achieving Compliance	40
Assistance from Compliance Function	41
Additional Check for Compliance	41
Compliance Audit	41
The Importance of Training	42
Selection of Employees to Participate	42
Senior Management Participation	42
New Employees	42
Establish Records of Compliance Activities	43
Review of Compliance Activity Records	43
Risk Management Advice	44

General

The goals of the compliance program for any financial institution's compliance function should be:

- To achieve maximum feasible compliance with the laws and regulations governing the financial institution;

- To prepare for the changes in regulation and compliance reporting required by legislative and regulatory amendments;

- To prepare for the changes in regulation and compliance reporting required by any business or geographic expansion; and

- To document and demonstrate the compliance efforts and commitments of the financial institution, its officers, and its employees.

Compliance Officer

For most institutions, a Compliance Officer should be the head of the compliance function. The Compliance Officer should report directly to senior management.

To assure consistent attention to compliance matters, we recommend that a financial institution give compliance responsibilities to someone within each operating division. The Compliance Officer will consult and coordinate activities with the compliance designee in each operating division.

Compliance Committee

A Compliance Committee should be established to advise the compliance function, just as other committees advise other functions within the financial institution. The Compliance Committee can be organized as either a board or a management committee. In either instance others within the institution with compliance responsibilities should be involved as members or advisers. These individuals include the internal auditor, the controller, the legal officer, and management officials with operational responsibilities.

Support for Senior Management

As its principal duty, the compliance function should support management in compliance matters. This support includes:

- Advising on the assignment of compliance responsibilities;

Organization and Duties of a Compliance Function 39

- Designing and managing a program of internal compliance reporting, including an annual compliance certification;

- Reporting regularly on compliance issues;

- Calling attention to significant new developments or requirements; and

- Coordinating educational and training programs.

Support for Operating Management

The compliance function should support operating management through:

- Reviewing operating policies and procedures;

- Recommending or reviewing systems to monitor compliance;

- Coordinating training programs;

- Identifying emerging issues or requirements and alerting operating management;

- Conducting compliance reviews to identify weaknesses, recommend enhancements, and monitor corrective actions;

- Advising management regarding the scope and procedures for compliance testing; and

- Maintaining and updating the Compliance Manual.

Senior Management Responsibility

Senior management is responsible for making compliance an integral part of a financial institution's operations and demonstrating compliance to regulatory authorities. Carrying out this responsibility includes:

- Establishing a compliance function and providing it with appropriate staff and resources;

- Assigning responsibility for complying with particular laws or regulations;

- Assuring that all managers are aware of their compliance responsibilities;

- Assuring that all operating policies and procedures adequately incorporate legal and regulatory requirements;

- Establishing internal compliance reporting systems;

- Identifying and correcting weaknesses in the compliance process;

- Documenting regular reviews of compliance issues;

- Communicating with supervisory agencies about compliance and other regulatory matters; and

- Participating in high-level educational or training activities.

With compliance, as with many other operational and policy issues, senior management must lead the way and measure the results. While senior management can and should look to the compliance function for advice and assistance *in all compliance matters, the responsibility for compliance rests with senior management.*

Oversight of Operational Management's Compliance Activities

Key to an effective compliance program is senior management's insistence that each operating manager is accountable for compliance in his or her division. The means of demonstrating this insistence includes:

- Requiring each operating manager to appoint a compliance coordinator;

- Requiring periodic compliance reviews and an annual compliance certification; and

- Including compliance among the factors to consider during performance evaluations.

Primary Responsibility for Achieving Compliance

The responsibility for achieving compliance belongs principally to operating management, not to the compliance function. The compliance function may set overall policy, coordinate implementation, and monitor compliance, but

Organization and Duties of a Compliance Function

> The compliance function coordinates implementation, and monitors compliance, but operating managers must have the primary responsibility for actually achieving compliance.

operating managers must have the primary responsibility for actually achieving compliance. Operating managers should:

- Draft and secure financial institution management approval for policies and procedures that incorporate legal and regulatory requirements;

- Appoint and supervise departmental compliance coordinators;

- Identify and address compliance deficiencies or concerns;

- Monitor and respond to new developments and requirements;

- Review staff training programs;

- Review compliance status;

- Coordinate testing programs with the compliance and internal audit departments;

- Report periodically to senior management about compliance issues; and

- Certify annually that their offices are operating in accordance with all legal and regulatory requirements.

Assistance from Compliance Function

In discharging these responsibilities, operating managers will receive advice and assistance from the compliance function. That help should be substantial, especially in the compliance function's coordinating or conducting training programs.

Additional Check for Compliance

Because of the increased regulatory emphasis on compliance as a means of corporate governance, internal audit often is responsible for compliance testing. In that capacity, internal audit serves as an additional check to determine whether the institution is complying with legal and regulatory requirements.

Compliance Audit

To perform a compliance audit, internal audit should:

- Review and enhance its procedures for testing compliance;

- Consult with the compliance function and the appropriate operating manager to determine the scope of compliance testing to be conducted during the audit before the audit begins;

- Test for compliance and report the results; and

- Monitor the corrections of any deficiencies noted in its report.

The Importance of Training

A financial institution's compliance goals can only be achieved if all personnel have adequate training to help achieve those goals.

A financial institution should adopt a policy to require *all* personnel — senior management, operating management, and staff — to receive compliance training on a regular basis. This periodic training should be appropriate for each individual's position. The training also should be designed to keep each individual current with compliance matters and conscious of the importance of an effective compliance program.

Selection of Employees to Participate

The success of the compliance training program depends on the selection of the employees to participate. The compliance designee in each operating department will be responsible for selecting employees for compliance training in consultation with division managers.

In selecting employees for training, the division head and the compliance designee should consult regulatory examinations and internal audit reports. The reviewers should be alert to recurring deficiencies and deficiencies that have not been satisfactorily resolved, for they indicate specific compliance needs. The division head also should document recurring compliance questions raised by employees. Finally, the compliance designee should interview employees informally to determine their compliance interests and needs.

Senior Management Participation

Senior management participation in compliance training programs sets an example for the staff and helps to assure the continued success of the compliance program. Senior management must have a general understanding of branch-wide compliance requirements.

They must receive frequent status reports on compliance developments and regulatory requirements.

New Employees

Compliance training for new employees deserves special attention. Any orientation program must stress the importance of the compliance program and the employees' responsibility for its success.

Establish Records of Compliance Activities

As one of its continuing duties, the compliance function should maintain records on the financial institution's compliance activities including documentation of:

- Establishment and organization of the compliance function;

- Compliance function budget;

- Development of training programs for use in the financial institution or review of training available through other sources;

- Participation in compliance training programs by senior management and operational management;

- Development and maintenance of a compliance manual;

- Policies and procedures for periodic review of compliance activities;

- Establishment of a program to identify and report on emerging compliance issues;

- Resolution of specific questions brought to the compliance function by the operating departments of the financial institution;

- Reports by the financial institution's compliance officer to senior management; and

- Annual certification of compliance.

Review of Compliance Activity Records

When properly maintained and reviewed, the records will identify the strengths and weaknesses of the financial institution's compliance activities. With good documentation, the necessary changes will become easier to accomplish.

Just as important, the recordkeeping will serve the financial institution well in a period of increasing regulatory scrutiny. The financial institution will be able to demonstrate continuous attention to the applicable legal and regulatory requirements and continuous changes in financial institution activities to conform to those requirements.

Risk Management Advice

> The compliance function has an increasingly important role in a financial institution, in part because the regulators expect to see a well organized and effective compliance function.

The compliance function has an increasingly important role in a financial institution, in part because the regulators *expect* to see a well organized and effective compliance function.

The Do's of establishing and operating a compliance function:

- Do make the compliance officer as senior as possible. Seniority indicates to the regulators that management is committed to an effective compliance program. In addition, because of the position in a hierarchy, a senior officer is more likely to be able to effect any required changes;

- Do make compliance training a high priority. Training is strong evidence of management's commitment to compliance;

- Do lead by example. Senior management should set the tone for the institution. Therefore, senior management should include the compliance function in many of the institution's processes and should regularly seek the advice of the compliance function;

- Do stay current with new developments. The compliance function should be aware of rules and policy changes and should communicate them to management and staff; and

- Do correct regulatory criticisms before the next examination. Regulatory criticisms increase in severity with repeated or uncorrected violations. The compliance function should be in a position to coordinate the institution's response to examination criticisms.

The Don'ts of establishing and operating a compliance function:

- Don't make the internal auditor the compliance officer. Regulators view the two roles as conflicting;

- Don't let the compliance manual fail the white glove test. If the financial institution has a compliance manual, it should be used and up to date. It should not be gathering dust on a shelf;

- Don't let compliance be leaderless. A committee may advise the compliance function, but a committee should not serve as the compliance function; and

- Don't assign the compliance officer role to a very junior individual. Neither senior management nor operating management is likely to heed the advice of the compliance officer when that officer holds a very junior position in the institution's hierarchy.

V. Examination Management

The Regulatory Examination Process 48

Examination Objectives 48

Examination Procedures 49

Preparing for and Managing Examinations 49

The Regulatory Examination Process

The federal financial regulatory agencies — the Comptroller of the Currency (OCC), Federal Reserve Board (FRB), Federal Deposit Insurance Corporation (FDIC), and the Office of Thrift Supervision (OTS) — have adopted generally uniform objectives and procedures to examine the financial institutions subject to their supervision.

Differences in examination philosophy and style still exist among the agencies, but the agencies are increasingly uniform. The trend toward uniformity began with the establishment of the Federal Financial Institutions Examination Council as a result of legislation in 1978. Congress has assured continuation of the trend with each new comprehensive law dealing with financial institution regulation during the 1980s and 1990s.

Examination Objectives

The agencies' common objectives in conducting their on-site safety and soundness examinations are to:

- Determine compliance with applicable laws and regulations;

- Determine the adequacy of the institution's written policies and procedures and the degree of the institution's compliance with them;

- Determine the adequacy of the financial institution's systems of records and internal controls;

- Evaluate the work performed by internal and external auditors;

- Assess management's expertise and ability to manage the institution's affairs;

- Assess the board of directors' oversight and ensure that management and the board are receiving complete and accurate reports;

- Assess the financial institution's ability to meet its future needs (e.g., fund growth, provide capital, absorb losses); and

- Identify any actual or potential undue risk to the institution.

The examiners write their examination findings in a report, a copy of which is given to the financial institution's management. The report will include:

- Analysis and conclusions regarding the institution's overall condition, trends, and prospects for the future;

- Discussions of the examiners' concerns about material risk to the financial institution's safety and soundness; and

- Recommendations for corrective action, when needed.

The agencies also conduct specialized examinations of trust activities, consumer compliance, and information systems. The examiners conducting the specialized examinations also will review a financial institution's performance and note areas for improvement using procedures and reports developed for the specialized examinations.

Examination Procedures

The agencies generally follow a series of common examination procedures often referred to as the "top-down approach." Under this method of examination, the examiners' initial focus is to review the institution's written policies and procedures and the extent to which its practices conform with those policies and procedures. The next focus of the examination is an analysis of the institution's documents such as loan files, management reports, and supporting financial records.

Examiners will conduct detailed testing if they determine that they cannot rely on the work done by the internal and external auditors.

Preparing for and Managing Examinations

The First Day Letter

In advance of the start of the examination, the examiners will send to the financial institution a "First Day Letter" listing the materials they expect to have available to them on their arrival at the start of the examination. The First Day Letter is a comprehensive document request and a financial institution's response to it can color the entire examination for the institution. A full and coordinated response to the First Day Letter will help with relations with the examiners and protect the institution.

We recommend that an institution gather as much of the requested documents as it can and put them in the room the examiners will use. The institution should prepare a list of the documents provided and match each document or file with a specific request in the First Day Letter.

Documentation Is King

Following a top-down examination, the examiners generally will not test or verify individual transactions. However, they will review a number of files for consistency with policies and procedures. They will usually review:

- Files that have been the subject of examination criticism in the past;

- Files that the financial institution has subjected to internal criticism; and

- Files in areas of new or unusual activity.

To manage this aspect of the examination, a financial institution should install sound quality control activities. Its records should be consistent with policies and procedures (all required documents in the file and current). For each type of activity, files should be consistent. Every loan file should include a summary sheet and all required documentation in the same order.

Appoint an Examination Coordinator

To manage the examination effectively, the financial institution should appoint an examination coordinator. The examination coordinator should take charge of compiling and organizing the documentation that responds to the First Day Letter. Later, during the examination, the examination coordinator should continue to serve as the document control person for the institution.

If the examination coordinator does not come from the compliance function, the compliance function should be involved in preparing for and managing the examination. Compliance is an important part of any examination, whether it is the general safety and soundness examination or a specialized consumer or trust examination.

In addition, the examination coordinator should be the liaison between the examiners and management. Centralizing communications will enable management to assure that examiners questions are answered accurately and completely and will provide better intelligence about the direction of the examiners' thinking.

Interviews and random employee questioning are common examination procedures. The examination coordinator should be aware of interviews and random questioning as well as the more formal aspects of the examination, such as file reviews and policy and procedure reviews.

The examination coordinator should visit daily with the examination team and attend to examiner needs. In doing so, the institution will improve the efficiency of the examination by being more responsive to the examiners' information requests. The institution will avoid the surprise of its own information and reduce the likelihood that examiners into an unanticipated area as a result of their own independent search for information or documents. In addition, the institution can improve its relationship with the examiners if it manages this daily contact well.

Information Flow

With the examination coordinator managing the examination for the institution, the institution can better document the flow of information to the examination team.

The examination coordinator should be responsible for keeping a log of all documents the financial institution has supplied to the examination team. The log should include information compiled in response to the First Day Letter as well as information supplied later. The examination coordinator may wish, in some circumstances, to require examiners to sign for files and periodically verify their return. In addition, the examination coordinator should keep a record of employee interviews.

The recordkeeping involved in this process has a twofold purpose. It will reduce the incidence of lost files. The recordkeeping will also give management and staff a record of their responses in the event of any dispute over information supplied to the examination team.

The Importance of Training

Training activities are tangible evidence of an institution's commitment to compliance. In managing an examination, a financial institution should document its training activities. As noted elsewhere in this *Handbook*, the training program should affect all levels of employees and should be designed to keep them current in areas of their responsibility.

The training aspect of examination management is one that could be easily overlooked. The examination coordinator should have documentation ready for the examiners showing recent training that officers and staff have attended since the last examination. In having this record, the financial institution will be able to show, in addition to its commitment to compliance, a consistent effort to keep current with professional and business developments and a consistent effort to maintain high levels of skills among officers and staff.

Correct Prior Exceptions

The exceptions can come from several sources including:

- Prior examination reports:
- Internal audit reports;
- External audit reports; and
- Reports from the compliance function.

Examiners will always review the previous examination report and consider whether the financial institution has responded appropriately to criticisms. Thus, to manage the examination properly, a financial institution must document its response to those criticisms. In most instances, it should be able to show it has made the appropriate correction. Where the process is not complete, it should show correction is under way. Lack of action usually assures more severe criticism of the uncorrected problems.

Examiners usually will consider the criticisms coming from the internal and external auditors and the compliance function. The financial institution should be able to document a response to these criticisms.

Know Your Stuff

Management and staff—and especially the examination coordinator—should be aware of the institution's policies and procedures. New policies and procedures are a focus of the examiners, and the institution's management and staff should be especially careful to be current with changed or new policies and procedures.

Compliance control points within the work flow are also a focus. Management should be aware of these control points and should be able to discuss them with the examiners.

Treat the Examiners Like Customers

Treating the examiners like customers is a simple solution to good examination management. Here are three points that are key to treating examiners like customers.

- Provide comfortable work space and sufficient equipment and materials;
- Supply information in an organized fashion and in a timely manner; and
- Make time for the examiners' questions.

> New policies and procedures are a focus of the examiners; the institution's management and staff should be especially careful to be current with changed or new policies and procedures.

VI. Information Systems

Introduction	54
Organization of IS Operations	54
Internal and External Audit	55
Management	57
Systems Development and Programming	60
Computer Operations	67
Information Systems Security	73
Data Integrity	81
Business Recovery Planning	85
Electronic Funds Transfer System	91
Internal Controls for Retail EFTs	98
End-User Computing and Networks	101
Document Imaging	106
References	107

Introduction

> Strong IS controls are essential for an effective risk management program.

Information systems (IS) is a key area of potential operations risk within a financial institution. Thus, strong IS controls are essential for an effective risk management program. An institution's IS environment may include service bureaus, facilities management sites, in-house data centers, and end-user computers working together to meet information processing needs. Institutions should review IS controls in each of these areas to ensure the accuracy and reliability of records and information resources.

IS examiners primarily focus on transaction risks, which are the risks associated with service or product delivery, and with providing support in all management processes (e.g., information for decision making and financial control). Transaction risk is present in all products, services, and aspects of an institution's operations (including at vendor locations).

> Financial institutions should establish effective internal controls and management information systems to safeguard information and measure operating performance and profitability.

Financial institutions should establish effective internal controls and management information systems to safeguard information and measure operating performance and profitability. Examiners from the federal financial institution regulatory agencies evaluate the internal control systems affecting the integrity, reliability, and accuracy of data. The IS examination also includes a thorough review of the effectiveness of management information systems and technology.

Organization of IS Operations

To ensure that an institution has a well-managed IS operation, management should address a number of different areas, including:

- Internal and external audit;

- Management;

- Systems development and programming;

- Computer operations;

- Information systems security;

- Data integrity;

- Business recovery planning;

- Electronic funds transfer systems;

- End-user computing and networks;
- Internal controls for retail EFTs; and
- Document imaging.

Internal and External Audit

Required Annual Independent Audits

Through the Federal Deposit Insurance Corporation Improvement Act (FDICIA), Congress required certain institutions to conduct an annual independent audit. (For a discussion of FDICIA requirements, see the Audits and Accounting Standards section in *The Commercial Banking Regulatory Handbook*.) As part of the management report required under FDICIA, management must include an assessment of the effectiveness of the internal control structure and procedures. Management, in preparing the assessment, and the auditor, in attesting to the financial statements, must consider the adequacy of IS controls. Therefore, establishing and using adequate internal controls in data processing is essential for a sound IS operation.

A well-designed internal control structure will assure senior management that:

- Records are processed accurately in a safe and sound manner;
- Accounting data are reliable;
- Operating procedures are efficient and effective;
- Procedures are in effect to assure continuity of services; and
- There is adherence to management standards and policies, applicable laws and regulations, regulatory policy statements, and other guidelines.

To ensure effective maintenance of these controls, an institution should perform an independent audit. (For a discussion of management's responsibility on internal and external audit generally, see the Internal and External Audit section of this *Handbook*.) An institution's board of directors is responsible for providing an adequate independent audit. If the institution's operations include data processing, the board should provide an internal or external audit to evaluate IS controls.

Role of the Internal Auditor

Internal auditors should play a major role in IS operations. Auditors evaluate the day-to-day IS controls to ascertain whether transactions are recorded and processed in compliance with acceptable accounting methods and the standards set by the board of directors and senior management. Auditors should also participate in the design, implementation, and testing of new IS systems and procedures.

Scope and Frequency of IS Audit Coverage

The scope of the procedures and frequency of internal auditing should be sufficient to accomplish the audit objectives established by internal audit. Covered areas include:

- *Compliance review* - Adherence to established policies, standards, and procedures;

- *Quality review* - The quality of formal policies, standards, and procedures, and the quality of management, efficiency of operations, and the adequacy of procedures and controls; and

- *Integrity review* - Fraud detection and deterrence, application program and operating system integrity, application system design and implementation, and monitoring employee activities.

Within these categories, auditors should review various functions, including reconcilements, data entry control, computer operations, systems development, program change, data communications, output distribution, and user department data processing controls.

Auditors should cover all areas of IS operations within an approved audit cycle. Because audit frequency and scope should be determined based on the inherent risk in an operation or application function, auditors will review some activities more frequently than others.

Audit Participation in Application Development and Testing

In addition to conducting scheduled IS audits, internal auditors should participate, from the beginning, in application development to ensure that applications incorporate effective controls. As an application reaches each state of the systems development life cycle, the auditor may review internal controls and audit trails included in the application.

Once a new application system or major revision to an existing system is accepted for production processing, the IS auditor, within the first year of production, should schedule a postimplementation review. By performing the review soon after conversions to production, auditors can identify and resolve processing errors or other unsatisfactory conditions. Internal audit's participation throughout the systems development life cycle should help minimize potential redesign costs or losses from processing errors or ineffective software controls. (For more discussion on the systems development life cycle, see the Systems Development and Programming segment in this section of the *Handbook*.)

External Auditors

When auditing an institution's financial statements, external auditors may review IS internal control procedures as part of their overall evaluation of internal accounting controls. CPA standards require an auditor to consider the effects of IS activity in each significant information systems accounting application.

Management

New and enhanced information systems and technology have enabled institutions to move data processing resources from centralized mainframe computers to distributed processing networks throughout the organization. Third-party vendors also offer a variety of financial products and services to replace or supplement in-house information systems. As a result, an institution may perform information processing using a combination of mainframe computer systems, service bureaus, and end-user computing systems. Due to this changing environment, the federal financial institution regulatory agencies and the industry are shifting their emphasis from the management of data centers to the management of information systems and technology.

Proper and effective management supervision is essential for the integrity of financial reporting systems and management information systems (MIS). A well-designed organization has:

> Proper and effective management supervision is essential for the integrity of financial reporting systems and management information systems.

- An effective management oversight structure;

- Clearly defined corporate IS policies and standards; and

- MIS that meets an institution's decision and reporting needs.

As in other areas of an institution, basic internal control principles such as segregation of duties, dual custody, and audit trails are key elements in IS controls.

Organization

The IS function should be an integral part of a financial institution's organizational structure. It should be an independent unit with the senior IS manager reporting to an institution's highest level of management.

All levels of an institution's management should be involved in IS for the organization to be effective. The board of directors should approve IS plans, policies, and major expenditures, and board members should be familiar with information systems and data center concepts and activities. Senior management is responsible for ensuring that the institution follows the board's policies and that the IS unit meets the institution's needs. IS management supervises the day-to-day activities, which requires a high level of technical proficiency.

Planning

To ensure that an institution's information systems meet future needs, management should continue to define long-term and short-term goals and objectives, and methods to achieve them. The board of directors and management should also integrate IS resources into the overall management or business planning process.

Management also may wish to form a high-level IS steering committee to serve as a general review board for major IS projects. The committee, whose members include representatives of senior management, the IS department, major user departments, and internal audit (participating in an advisory capacity), would oversee the development and maintenance of the IS strategic plan. It should not become involved in routine operations.

Policies and Procedures

Written policies, procedures, and standards provide the basis for establishing and maintaining proper IS controls. Written standards promote uniform implementation of management policies and aid in training new employees. Management should provide policies and procedures for operating units within the IS department. These policies should provide each unit with the necessary guidelines to coordinate and perform their tasks effectively in accordance with the overall polices and procedures of the organization and the IS department.

Internal Controls

Management is responsible for establishing an effective system of internal controls. When internal controls are applied to automated systems, they are classified into general and application controls. General controls are part of the information systems environment and include controls over data center operations, system software acquisition and maintenance, access security, and application systems development and maintenance. They apply to all systems, mainframes, minicomputers, and end-user computing. They control the modification and maintenance of computer programs, operating system software, and access to applications and data maintained on computer systems.

Application controls, which are specific to each application, are designed to protect the integrity of the application software by detecting and correcting errors when data are entered into the system. They ensure the authority of data origination, accuracy of data input, integrity or processing, and verification and distribution of output.

Management Reporting

Management reporting that measures the performance of information systems operating units and data centers is another step in the control process. Reporting may be separated into different functional areas for convenience such as: (1) operations, (2) systems development and programming, and (3) general and personnel. The types of information and frequency and sophistication of reports will vary depending on the size and nature of the IS department.

Management reporting also helps management identify deviations or exceptions from expected performance. Although establishing controls is within the purview of management, internal and external auditors should specify areas in which the controls are inadequate.

Insurance

Management should ensure that the institution carries adequate insurance to cover IS-related losses. In determining the amount of insurance, management should consider where it is exposed to loss, the extent of which insurance is available to cover potential losses, and the cost of insurance. Management should weigh these factors to determine how much risk the institution will assume directly. In assessing the extent of that risk, management should analyze the impact of uninsured loss both on the entity that incurs the loss and on the affiliates and the parent. Insurance should cover, among other things, potential losses arising from:

- Errors and omissions of the institution;

- Employee infidelity;

- Data lost during transportation to off-site facilities; and

- Electronic funds transfer systems.

Once management has acquired appropriate coverage, it should establish procedures to periodically review the insurance program to ensure the continued adequacy of coverage. The board of directors should annually review the insurance program.

Outsourcing Data Processing Services

Rapid changes in information systems technology have significantly increased the costs of developing and maintaining in-house and end-user information systems. As a result, many financial institutions have contracted with third-party organizations for data processing, telecommunications, item processing, or other selected services. These arrangements are generally referred to as outsourcing. The primary goal of outsourcing is to reduce operating expenses by removing salary and equipment expenses from the institution's books and allocating the savings in capital to core business needs.

Outsourcing arrangements permit an institution to focus on its primary business and rely on the servicer to provide state-of-the-art systems that comply with regulatory requirements. Longer-term outsourcing contracts also permit the institution to predict its data processing costs with a higher degree of certainty, as the servicer bears the costs of technological changes. The vendor achieves cost savings and economies of scale by consolidating and reducing data processing facilities, computers, and software maintenance activities. When developing long-term outsourcing contracts, management should ensure that the contract facilitates management's strategic plans.

Emerging Technologies

The proliferation of emerging technologies in information processing exposes institutions to new risks including: increased volume of data; increased speed of processing; more online reporting capabilities; more complex business processes; and more user-controlled processing. These changes have: increased user access to information systems; reduced segregation of duties; shifted from paper to electronic audit trails, reduced standards and controls for end-user systems; and increased the complexity of business recovery planning.

Systems Development and Programming

Management should ensure that written standards and procedures provide guidance for all IS processing functions within a systems development or maintenance process. Standards should address systems design, programming, testing, systems implementation, documentation, and software maintenance. They should include guidelines for effective project controls and procedures for reviewing and acquiring software systems.

Systems and programming standards should:

- Identify control procedures to ensure program integrity;
- Restrict unauthorized access; and
- Provide for adequate systems documentation.

The IS processing procedures should identify physical restrictions, software control, and accounting controls required to maintain security within the application systems, operating systems, and data files.

Program documentation is one of the most vital and neglected areas of information systems, and management should actively participate in developing appropriate standards for documentation. Proper documentation creates an accounting of both the essential elements of the information systems application and the logic of the computer software programs. It is the basic source of information for those who audit, correct, improve, manage, operate, or use the system.

> Program documentation is one of the most vital and neglected areas of information systems, and management should actively participate in developing appropriate standards for documentation.

Project Control

The process used to control projects for systems and applications development, acquisition, or revision is a key factor for maintaining a well-managed IS facility. Management should closely monitor systems development to control costs and ensure the creation of well-structured applications.

A project control system should employ well-defined and proven techniques for managing projects and generating application development records. The system should, at a minimum, contain:

- Target completion dates for each task or phase of systems development;
- Measurement of progress against original target dates; and
- Project control data aids to assist in managing the system and programming function.

Systems Development Standards

Written standards and procedures should govern each activity, including:

- System design;
- Software analysis and selection;

- Programming and testing;
- Implementation;
- Cataloging;
- Modifications; and
- Documentation.

System Design and System Development Life Cycle

The systems development life cycle (SDLC) is a common approach to managing application software. It identifies the sequence of activities required in the systems development process and throughout the useful life of an application.

An application system's life cycle is completed as replacement systems are implemented. Management should establish and approve standards for each phase of the development process. Management may better plan, implement, and maintain software systems through use of a corporate SDLC. The major components of an SDLC should include:

- *Project initiation.* The initial phase of the systems development process addresses conceptual changes and determines the feasibility of pursuing further development;

- *Requirements definition.* The requirements definition converts the system concepts into detailed specifications. The analysis and specifications should clearly identify user needs and expectations within the proposed application; and

- *Systems design.* Systems design involves the conversion of user requirements into specifications for programming and implementation. Users should participate in the system design to ensure that the application design will meet their needs. Systems design techniques should detail the sequence of program flow, the files to be used, the reports to be produced, and the controls to be built into the system.

Software Analysis and Selection

Financial institutions of all sizes are finding that purchasing software is a cost-effective alternative to developing software systems in-house. Vendors can also provide the necessary technical expertise for continued support of these products. Management should establish written standards for evaluating vendor software and for guiding the selection process.

Programming and Testing Standards

Management should develop written standards that establish appropriate controls and procedures for the programming and testing phases. To ensure that the application will process data correctly and produce reliable output in the desired format, management should conduct tests using predetermined data under controlled conditions. Management should develop strict standards to govern the testing process. Standard testing procedures should require:

- A documented test plan;

- A parallel test of new application systems. (This output can then be compared with existing output to determine processing validity.);

- Independent verification of test results by user representatives;

- A control mechanism to prohibit programmers and end-users from using live data files for testing, training, and demonstrations;

- The simulation in test data of all possible error conditions to ensure that the program effectively handles all situations; and

- A thorough test of any changes to existing programs.

Implementation and Evaluation

An institution should also have written standards for implementing software changes and new systems to ensure that they are ready for production. Implementation standards should require:

- Documented acceptance of the application system by users and the computer operations department;

- Complete user and operator run manuals describing each of the processing steps;

- System training for all users and computer operators; and

- Complete documentation before implementation.

Management or internal audit should conduct a postimplementation review after the application has been operational for a short time. Reviewers should interview all parties actively involved with the system's operation and note any specific problems.

Program Modification

Some modification of information systems programs will be necessary during the application life cycle. Program changes should be strictly controlled and documented to prevent fraudulent or inadvertent modification.

Requests for program changes should be documented on a standard change request form. Both management and the programming unit review and approve change requests. This process allows each unit to be aware of pending changes and clarify the specific request. The form should include a description of the request and document the review and approval process. It should provide an accurate chronological record of the description of all changes to production programs. Copies of the program change forms should ordinarily be distributed to the requester, the system user, and the programming unit. Depending on the internal control process, the audit department either may require a copy or have access to copies.

Management should establish strict procedures to control the movement of modified programs into the production environment. These procedures should identify:

- Security of programs before placing them into production;

- The approval process required to promote programs to production; and

- The personnel responsible for placing programs into production.

Control procedures for modification of operating systems should parallel those for changes to application programs.

Occasionally, management must bypass the normal change procedures to change a program, such as a change required to restore production processing. Supervisory personnel should strictly control temporary changes to prevent unauthorized changes and to ensure that approved changes are made correctly.

Programming Personnel

Management should develop and enforce written standards to monitor and control all programming activities, giving special emphasis to segregation of duties for all levels of programming personnel. A clear distinction between the application programming and systems programming duties should exist.

- *Application programmers.* Management should clearly define the activities of application programmers and should restrict access to programs outside the programmers' individual responsibility. Management should also assign maintenance responsibilities to specific programmers for each major application. Programmers not assigned to maintain or develop specific programs should have restricted access to those programs; and

- *System programmers.* System programmers are a distinct group of highly skilled programmers responsible for maintaining operating systems, teleprocessing control systems, and database systems and for developing supportive applications.

Program Security

Management should maintain strict physical and logical security over access to and use of computer programs. Procedures should restrict unauthorized access to:

- Application programs;

- Operating systems programs;

- Data files;

- Documentation; and

- Computer equipment.

In addition, management should periodically review activity logs, time records, and other reports. Management may use system utility programs that flag exceptions. Those utility programs may also be used to alter storage, data files, and object code; enter the supervisor state; and catalog, delete, and rename programs. Management should prevent unauthorized use of these utility programs.

Documentation Standards

All institutions should include procedures and requirements for developing and retaining program documentation. Well-documented systems are easier to maintain and convert to new systems. Good documentation also facilitates the rotation of personnel and separation of duties and supports the continuity of operations in the event of key personnel turnover.

Developing and documenting standards requires analysis of the institution's current IS environment and projections of future requirements by the institution and IS management. When documentation is complete, management should implement plans to update and revise documentation as the institution's needs become more sophisticated and diverse. If an institution allows end-users to modify programs from microcomputer or LAN systems, the institution also should specify the level of user documentation that is required.

To ensure that documentation is properly maintained and easily accessible, management should assign the function of documentation librarian to one individual. The librarian should be responsible for the control, retention, storage, and distribution of master documentation files. Standards for documentation should specify the authority and techniques for maintaining and controlling program documentation.

User Manual Documentation

User manuals enable the user to understand, approve, and operate the system. Continuing user involvement is of primary importance; therefore, user aids or manuals are essential aspects of program documentation. Management should formally establish the responsibility and standards for writing user manuals.

Data Security and Privacy Mechanisms

Data security denotes protecting data against accidental or intentional disclosure to unauthorized persons or from unauthorized modification or destruction. Privacy concerns the rights of individuals about whom information is stored in a database. The seven essentials of data security are:

- Data should be protected from fire, theft, and other physical hazards;

- Data should be reconstructible to recover from destruction or loss;

- Data should be auditable for prompt detection of loss;

- The system should be tamperproof to prohibit programmers from bypassing controls;

- Users should be identified before being granted access;

- The system should be able to check that user actions are authorized; and

- User actions should be monitored so that suspicious or underauthorized behavior can be investigated.

To protect data best from misuse, an institution should have a database administrator. The administrator has a number of functions, including:

- *Defining data* (e.g., naming data items types, detailing data items in the data dictionary, establishing standards for data records and files used by programmers, and establishing retention periods);

- *Designing a database* (e.g., physical structuring of data on media, developing access methods, and developing security measures and techniques for maintaining privacy);

- *Operating data* (e.g., investigating all data errors, supervising restart and recovery operations, controlling and documenting changes to the database, and educating users); and

- *Security* (e.g., investigating all known security violations, investigating suspicious activity noted on exception reports, establishing an authorization hierarchy, modifying security codes, monitoring compliance with security procedures, and conducting periodic security audits to test compliance).

For the most effective risk management, the institution's management should separate the database administrator's duties from other IS functions. Although the administrator is the guardian of an installation's information, the administrator should not have access to application-related data. Management should also control access to source listings and other application program documentation.

Database Monitoring

An essential feature of a database system should be adequate transaction logs or journals. These logs should be detailed enough to facilitate recovery from minor hardware failures, software failure, and incidents where database files have been damaged or destroyed. They should include the application transactions and the administrative and operator messages accompanying the transmission during processing.

In addition, a log or journal provides an audit trail to trace the history of a transaction and investigate the cause of an error. The log can also highlight system utilization and data and procedural violations that may indicate security breaches.

Computer Operations

The computer operations department is generally responsible for selecting, operating, and maintaining the computer and telecommunications equipment that retains and processes an institution's information assets. The department should maintain a stable production environment, process the data promptly and efficiently, and protect the data files, programs, and equipment under its control.

The computer operations department generally performs the following functions:

- Computer operations;

- Communications network control;

- Data preparation;

- Transaction processing;

- Workload scheduling;

- Media library maintenance;

- Documentation library maintenance;

- Performance monitoring; and

- Disaster contingency planning.

The controls described in this segment describe centralized computer facilities; however, the concepts also apply to end-user computing systems located throughout an organization.

To perform their job functions, computer operations personnel should have access to the information necessary to run the various equipment and programs. All information for processing work should appear in the operator's run manuals. The information should be limited to the functions to be performed and the hardware, software, and data files to be used for processing and maintaining the equipment. Run manuals normally include processing procedures, rerun instructions, special application instructions, file rotation procedures, recovery instructions, and emergency procedures. Computer operators should not have access to software and hardware documentation that is not necessary to perform their duties. Management, assisted by computer operations and systems development and programming personnel, should ensure that operator's run manuals are current.

Separation and Rotation of Duties

Operations management should implement policies and procedures for separating and rotating duties and cross-training personnel. Management should assign duties to separate responsibility for different elements of computer operations and application processing. Computer operators should not perform any duties other than those directly relating to equipment operation. However, this limitation is not meant to prohibit operators from learning other duties or from performing them in an emergency. For example, there should be no overlap between computer operations and data preparation for processing. Generally, computer operators should not perform duties such as reject reentry, general ledger balancing, or settling unpolluted items. Management should not allow an individual to perform one function from start to finish or to be responsible for checking the accuracy of his or her own work.

> Management should not allow an individual to perform one function from start to finish or to be responsible for checking the accuracy of his or her own work.

Rotation of duties serves as both an internal control and cross-training tool. Tasks and shift should be rotated among computer operators to provide each operator with training for operational tasks and to prevent operators from handling any one function for extended periods. Employees should be rotated for sufficient duration to permit disclosure of any irregularities.

In smaller institutions, where there is little separation of duties, rotating duties takes on added significance as an internal control measure. The actual rotation should be logged to document performance. When persons normally not responsible for furnishing the computer act as operators, management should closely control computer time and continually review any conflicting functions. As in other departments, management should require mandatory vacations of at least two consecutive weeks for all IS personnel.

Equipment Maintenance

Management should ensure that the computer operations department performs preventive maintenance on all equipment. This requirement includes minor maintenance as well as more extensive maintenance a manufacturer or vendor may provide. Operations should perform all maintenance according to a predetermined schedule, not on a random basis, recording all maintenance in logs or other records. Management review of these records will aid in monitoring employee and vendor performance. Where a manufacturer or vendor performs maintenance under contract, the agreement should provide for repair services, detail the preventive maintenance to be performed, and indicate a schedule for both.

Operators should maintain a written log of all hardware problems and downtime they encounter between maintenance sessions. A periodic report on the nature and frequency of those problems is a necessary management tool and may be valuable for vendor selection, equipment benchmarking, replacement decisions, or planning for increased equipment capacity.

Workload Scheduling

Computer workload scheduling is critical to efficient IS operations. A well-managed scheduling procedure will:

- Ensure efficient use of computer resources;
- Allow for the late arrival of input; and
- Assign an overall priority rating to all jobs.

Management should periodically receive system usage reports indicating scheduled and unscheduled production time, program test and assembly time, reruns, and maintenance. Variations from scheduled activity should be investigated.

Equipment Controls

Equipment controls are procedures that prevent or detect unauthorized program execution and computer usage. They consist of the console printer, internal CPU clock, and system activity logs. The console printer indicates communication between the operation and the machine, and the internal CPU clock allows the computer to show a time for each job initiated. System activity logs record communication between the computer and the operator and between different parts of the computer system.

Management also should implement certain minimum operating procedures:

- The computer room should not be left unattended while the computer system is in operation;
- At least two computer operators should be assigned to each shift where practicable;
- Operators should not be allowed unilaterally to override any hardware or operation system checks;
- Operations should be required to run all jobs according to the schedule to prevent unauthorized jobs from being run and to assure that all authorized jobs are run; and
- Only authorized personnel should run the equipment.

Operator Controls

Computer operators generally have access to programs and data on the system through the equipment and may exercise latitude in dealing with day-to-day processing. To establish an adequate level of security and internal control, specific rules should limit the scope of and properly direct operator activity.

Rules common to most computer centers are:

- Operators should not execute data or software-altering utility programs without proper authorization;

- Operators should not have access to source programs or program listings;

- Operators should not perform any balancing functions other than run-to-run controls;

- Operators should observe all security procedures, including proper library procedures; and

- Operators should initiate the execution of only those programs submitted in accordance with established data center procedures.

Library Controls

Library controls are procedures to maintain and prevent unauthorized access to data files, programs, and documentation. Any computer installation has several libraries. A physical library contains data and program files and also system and program documentation. The library containing the files should be a secure room where files can be stored adjacent to the computer room to facilitate the retrieval and storage of processing files. Operators should have restricted access to the library containing system and program documentation.

In addition to physical libraries, the computer system usually has several types of program and file libraries. There are generally three types of program libraries:

- *The test library* contains those programs or modules currently being modified or developed by the programming staff;

- *Production libraries* contain programs used to process the center's work; and

- *Private libraries* are sometimes used to retain software that does not conveniently fit the other two categories. The existence and use of private libraries should be addressed in installation standards and be closely monitored by operations management.

For each of these program libraries, IS management should retain both a source version and an object version of the library.

Lacking any restrictions, an operator can read, copy, execute, rename, delete, or replace a program from the computer system libraries. Because these program library maintenance functions should be restricted, many installations use a library software package for program library control. Library software usually performs a combination of the following functions:

- Restricts access to source (and possibly object) programs, often using a key or password that denotes the authority level of an individual user;

- Maintains on a separate file the date and time of access, type of operation performed (such as execute, copy, rename, and read), and identity of the individual (or program) that accessed the module; and

- Provides periodic printed reports of the previous and other information.

Some important considerations for controlling access to files and libraries in all installations are:

- Assigning specific responsibility for the maintenance of production libraries;

- Providing proper authorization to operations personnel to support any changes to production libraries;

- Denying operators access to magnetic media other than those required for processing application; and

- Prohibiting operators from executing programs from test libraries during production runs.

In addition to controlling access to files libraries, management should ensure adequate protection against physical hazards. Management should maintain backups in a separate building away from the data centers so that a disaster occurring at one location would not be likely to affect both sites.

Transaction Processing

A financial institution's basic business is receiving, recording, and process-

---

Generally, to maintain proper segregation of duties, an individual should not be responsible for any two of the following functions:

- Input preparation;
- Operating data input equipment;
- Operating computer and sorting equipment;
- Preparing rejects and nonreads for reentry;
- Reconciling output; and
- Distributing output.

ing customer transactions in an accurate, reliable, and timely manner. The integrity, reliability, and accuracy of data depend on the existence of proper control procedures throughout all phases of transaction processing. Whether the control procedures are manual, automated, or a combination of both, coverage should include transaction initiation, data entry, computer processing, and distribution of output reports. Internal transaction control considerations include:

- Input processing and output functions should be segregated;

- Overnight control of dollar totals for rejects and holdover items should be well-defined and effective;

- Work returned from processing should be reconciled and balanced to the previously established control totals;

- Exception items should be cleared in an expeditious manner (exceptions are contrary to effective control and create potential risk to the institution);

- Exception reports should be reviewed by key officers and operation supervisors; and

- All output should be produced, properly distributed, and controlled.

Information Systems Security

Information is one of the most important assets of an organization, and protecting or securing information and facilities that process and maintain information is vital to the continuity of operations. Information security poses serious risk management problems as deficiencies may result in lost business, damaged reputations, fiduciary losses, lost assets, and possibly lost trade secrets. Security controls safeguard information from unauthorized or accidental modification, destruction, and disclosure, and they ensure timeliness, availability, and usability of data. Possible threats to operations include ignorance and carelessness, fire and water damage, disgruntled or unethical employees, outsiders or hackers, and viruses.

Information security is intended to provide reasonable protection against the risks of unauthorized or unintended access to computer data and resources. The basic principles of information security are:

- *Confidentiality* - Only authorized users should have access to data. This access should be limited on a need-to-know basis. Users should have access limited to those functions necessary to complete their assigned tasks;

- *Integrity* - Access to data should occur in a controlled manner to ensure reliability; and

- *Availability* - All information systems should remain operational so individuals depending on the system can rely on its availability.

To support these basic security principles, management should develop an institution-wide information security strategy and provide for the following:

- *System integrity* - protection from unauthorized modifications to the operating systems;

- *Authentication* - system recognition of distinct, individual users combined with verification that the users are who they represent themselves to be;

- *Authorization* - a means of determining which specific actions a user will be permitted to perform under certain circumstances using specified system resources;

- *Data integrity* - limitation of user access rights to prevent unauthorized data modification;

- *Data privacy* - limitation of user access rights to prevent unauthorized disclosure of data; and

- *Auditability* - detection and reporting of attempts to breach security or to gain unauthorized access to sensitive resources.

A completely secure data processing system is neither practical nor economically feasible. The level of security and control provided within a given environment should depend on the nature of the information resources to be protected. Management should consider the potential impact to the business when determining the appropriate level of data security to balance the relationship between risk and cost.

Security Administration and Accountability

Management should regulate and monitor the computer environment by incorporating into normal business practices security standards, policies, procedures, and controls. Maintaining a secure environment requires vigilance. After management establishes a security plan, additional security procedures should ensure that employees follow the plan and that they quickly detect threats to the system.

A security administrator or information security personnel should be responsible for security. The security administrator or information security personnel should be familiar with the institution's overall security policies and should have the authority to recommend and implement controls in strategic areas. Personnel departments should be responsible for tracking all terminations. Depending on an institution's size, security measures can range from simple file scanning to full-scale surveillance of equipment and data files. Those security measures also may include issuing user identification codes, maintaining and establishing user security levels, and controlling access to sensitive data and program files. In general, security administration responsibilities should include:

- Performing risk analyses;

- Establishing, enforcing, and monitoring the security program for all platforms (mainframe, minicomputers, LANs, and microcomputers); and

- Acting as a liaison between users and management.

Security administration for a microcomputer may be different from that for a mainframe, minicomputer, and LAN.

Mainframe and LAN administration is centralized through the use of security software. Microcomputer software is implemented and administered on each individual unit. Because computers are widely distributed throughout an institution, the administrator may need to delegate immediate supervision to designated persons within user areas or assign a departmental security contact who is responsible for overseeing and coordinating the area's security requirements and controls. These individuals in turn would report security violations to the security administrator.

Overall Security Plan and Emergency Procedures

An overall security plan includes physical protection of the data facility and IS equipment throughout the organization. The plan should be developed with the approval and involvement of top management. The plan should cover all functions performed in the IS operation and all areas touched by automation. Senior management should emphasize its commitment to security and should provide for communicating security objectives to all employees.

Security of the IS operation should be integrated with the security plan of the entire organization, and capable senior officials should be charged with developing, implementing, and enforcing the plan at all levels. A well-developed security training program that includes instruction in the use of emergency equipment, periodic testing and drills, and regular review of security procedures will reduce the vulnerability of the organization. Properly trained IS auditors can independently assess the extent to which a formal security plan is being followed and may play a key role in assuring it adequacy.

Physical Protection of Facilities

For physical protection of the data processing facility and all computer equipment, management should adopt measures to minimize exposure or the probability of threat to all computer hardware and software throughout the organization. Management should rank computer resources in order of importance and protect them with a commensurate level of security. Management should identify the protection provided, the significance of specific threats, and the individuals responsible for executing the program. Management may wish to restrict access to the sensitive information about the security plan so that protection measures are not compromised. The plan should document:

- Steps to be followed during and immediately after an emergency; and

- Preventive and detective measures for other business interruptions, (e.g., those due to unauthorized access and manipulation of data and programs, and to inaccurate or incomplete processing).

Management should ensure that building security measures include surveillance equipment and procedures that permit only authorized people to enter the facility. Actual building security precautions will vary depending on size and location of the data center or institution. Employees who have access to secured areas should have proper identification, and all visitors should sign-in and wear proper IDs so they can be easily identified.

Contingency Planning

Backup and contingency planning is another critical element of the overall security program. To be effective, the plan should detail the procedures that management should follow to move the operations to an alternate site or to continue processing. In addition, the plan should include procedures for continuing business functions within other key departments that provide input to the operations. (For detailed discussion of contingency planning, see the Business Recovery Planning segment of this section of the *Handbook*.)

Microcomputer and Network Security

Physically securing computer equipment is also of vital importance to an institution's operations. A computer located in a user department is often less secure than one located in a computer room. Management should establish internal control procedures for all computers, regardless of the computer's size. The level of security surrounding any computer should depend on the significance of the applications processed and risks to the organization, the cost of equipment, and the availability of backup equipment.

Physical security for distributed data processing, particularly LANs, is slightly different from that for mainframes or minicomputers. A network may extend beyond the local premises and may not be located in a centralized computer room. As with the traditional mainframe or minicomputer environment, physical network security should prevent unauthorized personnel from accessing LAN devices or the transmission of media. Hardware, software, and data on removable media should also be protected.

Only the LAN administrator should have access to the network servers (files, applications, communications, etc.). Network workstations or microcomputers should be password protected and monitored for all workstation activity to prevent unauthorized personnel from accessing the LAN. Network wiring requires some form of protection, as it may reveal dates without being physically penetrated.

Data Security

In addition to protecting hardware, an institution should restrict access to software and data. The institution may incur considerable damage, including financial loss, if these valuable assets are lost, stolen, or compromised. Implementing and enforcing data security controls will protect the data and software resources against accidental or intentional disclosure to unauthorized persons or unauthorized modification or destruction. The seven essentials of data security are:

- Protect data from fire, theft, and other physical hazards;

- Be able to reconstruct data to recover from destruction or loss;

- Be able to audit data from prompt detection of loss as well as accidental and intentional manipulation;

- Make systems tamperproof to prohibit programmers and systems analysts from bypassing controls;

- Require the system to check the identity of users before granting them access;

- Ensure that the system has the ability to check that user actions are authorized; and

- Monitor user actions so management can investigate suspicious or unauthorized activity.

Deliberate or accidental security exposures present in all data processing environments may be heightened by certain features of automated systems. Deliberate threats include "trap-doors" left by a programmer, misuse of another person's authorized access code, obtaining access codes or other restricted data from hard copies of output left in trash cans, and obtaining access codes or other restricted data by wire-tapping. Accidental threats include faults in the data communication system leading to erroneous data in the database and failures in hardware or software that lead to a breakdown of a built-in security feature. For example, secret data, such as passwords, may be printed as part of a core dump during an abnormal termination or a recovery.

The accuracy and integrity of data as well as continued operations depend on an institution's having proper control procedures and guidelines for processing in both the user and data processing areas. To ensure that data are secure and operations are uninterrupted, management should review the following key elements of data security for all platforms (mainframe, minicomputers, LANs, and microcomputers):

- Logical access security;

- Data integrity;

- Telecommunications security;

- Output distribution controls;

- Virus protection strategy;

- User education; and

- Accountability.

Logical Access Security and Controls

Logical access security prevents unauthorized users from connecting or gaining access to application and system resources before and after achieving physical connection to microcomputers, local area networks, and minicomputer or mainframe systems. Logical access security includes logical access controls (user IDs and passwords) and programming security (systems software access).

Logical access security objectives should include identification and authorization of users. The degree of control necessary within each computer system depends on the system's use. Microcomputers can be used as stand-alone systems or as access links to mainframes, minicomputers, or LANs. In addition, management should differentiate computers that can access classified information and those that use only unclassified information.

Computer capability may be limited by function (e.g., read, write, execute, and allocate). Depending on the function and the sensitivity of the application or data, management may implement protection at the system database, file, record or field level. Wherever possible, management should limit user access to those functions necessary to perform a specific job.

A user ID grants initial access, and a password authenticates user authorization to access the system. Users should hold their passwords in strict confidence and should change passwords periodically or whenever they are compromised (i.e., voluntary or involuntary termination of employment). Passwords should be difficult to guess and adequately protected. Methods of protection consist of:

- Maintaining passwords in protected storage in an encrypted format;

- Using spring suppression, scrambling, or overprinting passwords when entered at the terminal;

- Printing decoys to camouflage the true password; and

- Limiting the number of attempts for accessing the system, (e.g., after three failures, the system denies the user access).

Departments within an institution should coordinate password administration and tracking. The security administrator should be responsible for maintaining user IDs and passwords. Personnel departments should accurately track all terminations and promptly notify the security administrator of all terminations. The security administrator should immediately remove access for all individuals who were terminated and modify access as necessary for individuals transferred to different departments.

System Logs

An individual other than the security administrator should regularly review system logs and exception reports for access violations. This division of responsibilities provides necessary checks and balances for managing systems security. Logs serve as an effective control in any online system and should include the following information:

- *Unauthorized log-in attempts.* The system should automatically record such attempts. The system should disconnect the offending terminal or microcomputer from the network and alert the responsible officer by displaying a message on the computer console or on a terminal display monitored by a security group;

- *Attempts to gain information above the user's level of accessibility.* The system should also automatically log these types of attempts. If a user continually attempts to access unauthorized information, the system should notify the responsible officer, who should investigate the multiple access attempts; and

- *A detailed transaction file for each application.* At minimum, this file should contain information about the transaction and identification of the terminal and operator that initiated the transaction. The system should maintain a separate transaction file for each accessible master file. As the system receives transactions from a terminal station, it should record the date, time, and sequence number in the file and then copy expanded transactions onto magnetic media. In some systems, the program acknowledges each transaction as it is received. If the system fails, the terminal operator should know the status of the current transaction at the time of failure.

Logs are also important for reconstructing the system after it fails. The transaction log may be used, if necessary, to reconstruct the master file by posting the entries in the transaction log to the backup master file. This posting will provide a detailed transaction file, aiding in security and also assisting with recovery in the event of an outage.

In addition to user IDs and password, logical access protection may be as simple as removing storage media (e.g., diskettes, tapes, removable hard drives) and keeping them in a secure location. Other controls include automatic logoff, time of day controls, keyboard locks, and data encryption.

Terminals or microcomputers used as stand-alones, terminal emulators, or networking devices utilize the security software on the desired platform for further controls after initial access has been granted. Once the user logs onto the system, different methods provide control, such as user profiles and authorization tables. User profiles are unique to each user and extend to programs, data files, terminals or microcomputers, time periods of access, and executable transactions and commands. Authorization tables involve classifying users into various groups with associated access levels. To reduce the likelihood of individuals circumventing system security controls, files containing user IDs, passwords, and log-on sequences should be assigned the highest level of security, permitting only limited access.

Unauthorized Disclosures

While user IDs and passwords protect against unauthorized access, they do not protect against unauthorized disclosures. Computers that are part of a network need further protection because they transmit data to other terminals or microcomputers (stand-alone and networked) as well as to mainframes or minicomputers. During transmission, all nodes can read traffic on the network, thus potentially compromising data.

Telecommunications security, such as data encryption, is required to assure data integrity, confidentiality, and system availability. While encryption is required to ensure the privacy of data during transmission, it can also be used to protect data files when other security mechanisms are unavailable and to protect files that are highly confidential.

Data Integrity

In addition to strong physical and logical access security, effective data integrity also requires input and processing controls. Proper use of such controls will improve data quality as well as processing efficiency.

In a distributed environment, data integrity is a greater risk and concern than with centralized mainframe systems because there are more opportunities to "transform" the data as they move through the various systems. This organization causes a number of potential problems, such as multiple copies of data and varying complex security access systems (i.e., more numerous, multilayered security environments to track the lack of mature security software in some environments, such as the LAN environment). Network systems that provide multiple users with access to shred data files and permit two or more users with access to shred data files to update the same files or records simultaneously create another data integrity concern. An institution should use software-locking mechanisms to prevent concurrent access.

Output Controls

An institution should control access to sensitive data, whether the data are displayed on a terminal monitor or on a report. Financial institutions and data processing centers have a significant amount of information in many forms—

printed and maintained in hard-copy format, stored and distributed via removable media, or displayed visibly on CRT terminals and other devices. Output controls should require an operator or supervisor to take a specific action before permitting sensitive data to print on a remote printer. Classified or sensitive data should not be printed automatically to a remote printer. The user should secure the output immediately.

Sensitive reports should never be left unattended by a copy or facsimile machine or on an individual's desk. Classified information should be secured in a locked desk or cabinet to prevent the possibility of theft, unauthorized disclosure, or modification. Management also should develop procedures for disposing of confidential data.

Telecommunications Security and Access Controls

Security of data communications is also a primary concern for all institutions that access a network or computer system from a nondirect link or remote location through satellite, radio microwave, or telephone line transmissions. Unauthorized dial-in access to mainframes, minicomputers, and LANs is a serious threat today. Management should ensure that an institution has controls in place to prevent threats to systems, applications, and data. Telecommunication controls generally are supplied for the terminals and files and for data transmission.

Identification and authentication features are fundamental controls. The system should know and verify the user, the type and location of the hardware, the date and time, the transactions attempted or performed and their status, and their data resources accessed. The systems may identify users through any combination of techniques that include a unique identification code (PIN); encoded cards, badges, encryption or verification keys, physical traits (e.g., voice or fingerprints); or passwords.

Identification and authentication of physical computers is especially important. Some computers can be identified by two levels of special identification numbers that are encoded internally. The lower level identifies the terminal or microcomputer. The system can verify these numbers automatically against a protected table of valid identifiers. The call-back method is another technique that validates computers after a user has signed on. The system disconnects the terminal or microcomputer and reconnects the line to a valid address. As an additional protective measure, management should adequately protect and periodically change phone numbers for dial-up systems.

Information Systems 83

Transmission Controls

Management should maintain special controls to protect the confidentiality and accuracy of transmitted data. Such controls may include:

- Parity checks;

- Message authentication;

- Encryption; and

- Error checking transmission protocols.

Although some institutions transmit data via satellite and microwave transmissions, telephone lines are the most common method of linking the remote user with a central processor, be it a mainframe, minicomputer, or LAN server. Because telephone lines are not maintained exclusively by the data center, management should develop physical and procedural controls to ensure that the system is both reliable and secure from outside penetration.

While communication line penetration is not easy, data communication systems are susceptible to exposure from line penetration or interception. The success of any attempt to penetrate a teleprocessing system depends on the perpetrator's technical knowledge of the data communications, the vulnerability of the targeted telecommunications system, and the accessibility to the necessary equipment. A telecommunications system is vulnerable to penetration or message interception through several methods.

- *Masquerading* - pretending to be an authorized user or repair person to gain access to the system (requires access to user identification and authentication codes);

- *Eavesdropping* - tapping or cutting in on telecommunications transmissions to monitor messages without interfering with them (requires access to identifiable communications lines or links);

- *Piggybacking* - monitoring transmitted messages to intercept, modify, or replace and then retransmit to the host computer or user; and

- *Line grabbing* - inserting a compatible terminal into the telecommunications line. The perpetrator eavesdrops on the line until the authorized user signs off; however, the perpetrator intercepts the sign-off message and prevents the message from reaching the host system. The perpetrator sends the user a false sign-off acceptance message and then has free access to the system.

Data transfers in a computer system should be made in a relatively error-free environment. However, when an institution transmits programs or vital data, management should use additional controls. Management may control transmission errors by error-detecting or error-correcting codes. The former are used more often because error-correcting codes do not correct all errors and are costly to implement. Generally, error-detection methods such as a check bit and redundant transmissions are adequate.

Redundancy checking is a common error-detection routine. The system checks a transmitted block of data containing one or more records or messages for number of characters or patterns of bits contained in the block. If the numbers or patterns do not conform with predetermined parameters, the receiving device ignores the transmitted data and instructs the user to retransmit it. The telecommunications control unit often adds check bits, which are similar to priority checks, to the transmitted data.

Checking techniques for detecting data transmission distortions have been proven to be effective. Implementing checking techniques in-house is very difficult if the equipment does not already have the capability. Therefore, management should consider error-detecting techniques when making purchasing decisions for teleprocessing network equipment.

Computer Viruses and Controls

In addition to the risk of transmission errors, an institutions' computer systems are susceptible to viruses. Viruses are computer programs that are unique in two respects. They can attach themselves to other programs, and they can replicate themselves and move to systems other than the one in which they were created. A user may not realize a virus is even in the code until the virus becomes active. The virus may perform harmless and obvious actions such as displaying a message, or it may trigger entirely random and serious actions, such as erasing parts of memory or erasing an entire hard disk.

Computer viruses most often occur on networks and microcomputers. Due to the complexity of the operating system and the security on mainframe computers there have been very few cases of computer viruses on mainframe computers. However, the increasing connectivity of computer networks and the trend toward more "open" systems magnifies the threat of viruses.

Management should implement controls, starting with a strong security policy, to protect systems against viruses. The policy should prohibit using untested or unlicensed software, loading software from bulletin boards, or using shareware that has not been validated. The policy should also prohibit copying of software and using personal software on the institution's microcomputers.

Viruses can infect a microcomputer through public software (shareware) loaded from the floppy drive or through programs transmitted from public electronic bulletin boards. One of the best ways to prevent viruses is to reduce the possible entry channels to a microcomputer. Preventive controls include:

- Prohibiting loading computer programs from public electronic bulletin boards or other untrusted sources. If these sources are necessary, load the program into an isolated computer until it can be tested adequately;

- ALWAYS using the writeprotect tabs on original diskettes before loading them into the computer for the first time;

- Making backups on a regular basis, being aware that even backups may be infected. Protect original disks, and do not leave them in open areas;

- Not permitting network users to access any outside bulletin boards without prior approval. Do not allow any transfer of executable programs over the network; and

- Scanning all new or foreign diskettes, including newly purchased software, for viruses before using them on a microcomputer.

User Education

Users have varying levels of expertise and familiarity with computers. Management should implement a user education program to promote awareness regarding proper use and care of computers and the user's obligation to challenge any person or procedure that may appear to violate the security of the automation or communication systems. Additionally, training should include all employees who use computers, and this training should be part of new employees' orientation. Training sessions should also be held during equipment installation.

In addition to regular training, accessibility of information is also an important aspect of user education. Operation and procedural manuals should be available to users at all times.

Business Recovery Planning

The main objective of business recovery planning is to provide for the development of comprehensive and useful procedures that will assist an institution with continuity and rapid recovery of business operations after an emergency or disaster. Effective business recovery planning typically addresses these five major areas:

- *Business impact analysis* - development of business recovery requirements that define business risks and recovery time frames;

- *Alternative strategy selection, backup, and analysis* - formulation and selection of cost-effective (commensurate with risks) recovery strategies to address short- and long-term interruptions;

- *Plan development* - development of detailed business recovery procedures addressing personnel, recovery resources, and recovery actions. Specifically, this objective covers identifying the individuals responsible for managing and performing the recovery process, defining and assigning team members' responsibilities, identifying key technical and nontechnical resources, and developing detailed restoration procedures;

- *Plan testing* - testing the business recovery plan to evaluate different components of the plan, identify problems, and implement resolutions; and

- *Evaluation and update* - periodic evaluation of the plan to assure that is being updated on a regular basis.

Business Impact Analysis

Management should perform a business impact analysis to establish the business functions that must be recovered to maintain the business and to determine the time frames in which these critical business functions must be recovered. This process should also identify threats to the business (e.g., earthquake, disk failure, loss of power) and evaluate current risk reduction measures that are in place or that need to be implemented). The results from this evaluation will determine which business functions must be recovered and how quickly they should be recovered.

Alternative Strategy Selection, Backup, and Analysis

After determining the business functions that must be recovered and how quickly they should be recovered, management should develop a recovery strategy. This strategy depends on the minimum resources needed to recover the critical business functions. Strategy options include:

- A "hot-site" recovery vendor, for a contractually agreed monthly subscription fee, provides an organization with space, hardware, and systems. This option is expensive but allows for the fastest recovery;

- A "cold-site" agreement provides an organization with space but does not provided hardware for recovery. Management must, thus, separately arrange acquisition of appropriate hardware and software. The "cold-site" is a less expensive option but does not provide for as quick a recovery as a "hot-site."; and

- Using space and processing capabilities at other locations within the organization.

The overall recovery strategy management chooses among these options should be based on the recovery time frames, the risks, the potential for loss, and the costs associated with recovery.

Potential misunderstandings may be avoided if an institution's management signs a formal written agreement with the backup site's management. The agreement should specifically identify the conditions under which the site may be used.

Written contingency procedures should, at a minimum, address:

- Conditions or situations that necessitate using the backup site;

- Responsibility for making a decision to use the backup and guidelines as to when management should make the decision;

- Employee notification;

- Backup site notification;

- Steps to be followed at the backup site; and

- Files, input work, special forms, and so on, to be taken to the backup site and means of transportation.

Management should assure that the backup site is tested at least annually and also when equipment is changed to ensure continued compatibility. To the extent practicable, operating procedures at the backup site should be established with a level of security protection comparable to that of the main data center and other IS operations outside the data center.

Software Backup

In addition to hardware backup, software backup is another important phase of business recovery planning. Software backup for all hardware platforms consists of three basic areas: operating system, application software, and documentation. All software and related documentation should have adequate off-premise storage. Even when using a standard software package from one vendor, the software will probably vary from one location to another. Differences may include interest rate modifications, reporting options, account applications, or other options chosen by the institution during or subsequent to system implementation. The more nonstandard an institution's software, the more critical it becomes to have off-site storage.

An institution's business recovery plan (BRP) should address storing, testing, and updating of operating system and application software. An institution should back up operating system software with at least two copies of the current version. Without the operating system software, even the most sophisticated computer hardware is useless. One copy should be stored in the tape and disk library for immediate availability in the event the original is impaired; the other copy should be stored in a secure, off-premise location. Management should ensure that duplicate copies are tested periodically and recreated whenever there is a change to the original.

Management also should retain backup copies of documentation for the operating system and the application programs. Management should maintain a minimum level of documentation at an off-site location, including current copies of:

- Operating system options and modifications;
- Application flowcharts;
- Descriptive narrative for all systems and programs;
- File layouts and transaction codes;
- Operator run instructions; and
- User manuals.

Procedure manuals are also necessary during disaster recovery. Management should store duplicate copies of all IS-related procedures at an off-site location. These copies include manuals on systems and programming standards, documentation, file libraries, computer operations procedures, and data control procedures. Most important, management should keep at an off-premise location a copy of the procedures outlining the IS emergency operation plans.

Data File Backup

The final and most important area of backup involves the institution's data files. Regardless of the platform in which data are located, an institution always should be able to generate a current master file. As with other backup files, management should retain copies of data files both on-site and off-site to provide adequate recovery capability. Retention of current data files, or older master files and the transaction files necessary to bring them current, is important so that processing can continue in the event of a disaster. Financial institution regulators consider a three-cycle retention the minimum acceptable standard for tape and serial-disk-oriented systems, while a two-cycle retention is normally used in direct-access-oriented systems.

As backup for each application, management should retain (both on and off the premises) the master files and transaction files sufficient to re-create the current day's master files. For applications that do not produce a daily master file, a cumulative transaction journal should be used and backed up in the same manner as master files.

Disk mirroring or disk duplexing is one means of providing on-site backup for all processing environments. These processes provide real-time backup of data to a secondary disk that can be used if the primary disk becomes nonfunctional. With mirroring, data and operations can continue immediately without any disruption to the user. Institutions using disk mirroring or duplexing systems should still retain off-site backups.

Telecommunications Backup

An effective BRP for telecommunications addresses the institution's communications media and equipment. The contingency plan should establish priorities (i.e., bank tellers versus ATMs, data versus voice lines, particular offices or sites, and transactions processed versus inquiries). The plan also should identify critical components of the network (e.g., if all lines in the building connect to a PBX and the building is serviced by a single cable to the telephone company central office, the plan should identify alternate routes to the backup central office). Rerouting and redundancy may permit the use of alternate equipment, facilities, lines, and circuits but may still be limited by other considerations, such as cost, the practicality of the selected backup components, and the security and data integrity provided by the backup plan.

Management should select alternatives suitable for the anticipated capacities at the speeds necessary to meet established priorities. The backup plan should recognize availability and lead times required to employ certain components, such as installing additional lines or modems and multiplexers at a backup site. Management should also consider reliability, flexibility, and compatibility, which are all considerations of the original planning process, in formulating the backup plan. Additionally, the telecommunications backup plan should be compatible with other contingency plans in the institution since it will affect users, data processing, and customers.

Plan Development

Management should require detailed procedures to recover both an institution's information systems components as well as its business units. These procedures should include: disaster declaration; call notification procedures; and network, operating systems, application, and database recovery procedures. In addition, these procedures should address where the business users will go and how lost work will be recovered.

The BRP should cover all of management's and staff's required actions during an emergency. In addition to containing recovery procedures for computer and network environments, the BRP should include procedures for performing operations manually that, under normal circumstances, are automated. Institutions should not rely solely on prompt recovery of systems.

Management's BRP should address protection against physical disasters and other disruption to operations, as well as backup considerations related to hardware, software, applications, documentation, data files, and telecommunications. Regardless of the type of computer equipment and software and the size of an institution's IS facilities, the BRP should also include insurance policies.

Plan Testing

A BRP is incomplete without regular testing. Management should revise and test the contingency plan annually. Strong preparation will enhance employee responsiveness, reduce confusion, and provide for logical decisions during a crisis.

Management should generally use progressive testing — that is, moving from smaller to more complete tests. However, to determine overall effectiveness of the business recovery plan, management should conduct real stress tests.

Evaluation and Update

Planning is a dynamic process requiring ongoing evaluation. Management should ensure that plans are updated and modified as circumstances dictate.

In assessing BRP costs, management should analyze the business impact (including cost or lost dollars), regulatory and legal requirements, and customer satisfaction. Management should weigh the costs of various alternatives against the extent of risk protection that each alternative provides. This as-

Information Systems

sessment also should address costs associated with testing, because all components of a plan should be tested periodically.

Electronic Funds Transfer Systems

Electronic funds transfers play a major role in both wholesale and retail payment systems. An electronic funds transfer (EFT) includes any transfer of funds initiated through an electronic terminal, telephonic instrument, computer, or magnetic tape so as to instruct a financial institution to debit or credit an account.

While we address wholesale and retail systems separately in this *Handbook*, certain regulatory concerns are common to both. For example, management should ensure that policies and procedures for all funds transfer activities adequately address the requirements of the Bank Secrecy Act and the Office of Foreign Asset Controls. (See the Bank Secrecy Act section of *The Consumer Banking Regulatory Handbook* and the Foreign Asset Controls section of *The Commercial Banking Regulatory Handbook*.)

Wholesale Electronic Funds Transfer Systems

Wholesale EFT systems, such as Fedwire and CHIPS, have become financial institutions' primary method for large-dollar ("wholesale") and "retail" payments. They are also an important and expanding element of "retail" payment systems.

The method an institution uses to generate payment instructions is critical to any payments system. A variety of electronic message networks that deliver payment instructions, including SWIFT, telex, and in-house data transmission terminals, support the systems. Payment instructions also may be generated by partially electronic or manual sources including telephone, fax, letters, memos, and standing instructions.

Payment Order Origination

The message systems customers use to originate payment orders are indispensible components of funds transfer activities. Unlike payments systems, message systems process instructions to move funds and administrative messages. The actual funds movement is accomplished by debiting the originating customer's account and crediting the beneficiary's account.

Because the payment order is the institution's authorization to act on behalf of the customer, an institution must have in place a system to establish the authenticity and time of receipt of the order. These two elements are the primary components cited by the Uniform Commercial Code Article 4A (UCC4A) in establishing responsibility for the execution of a payment order. UCC4A, which has been adopted by a majority of the states in the United States and incorporated into the Federal Reserve System's Regulation J, establishes liability for improper or untimely processing of a payment order, or cancellation, from initiation to final execution of the originator's instructions. Included in UCC4A is a requirement that financial institutions and their customers establish a security agreement that is acceptable to both.

Several phases exist in funds transfer operations where inappropriate or incorrect use of the system can occur. As a result, an institution needs a clearly defined authentication procedure throughout the process. Management should establish effective controls over the following areas:

- Original instructions from the customer to the financial institution;

- Every transfer point of data for each step of the manual process; and

- Every transfer point of data for each step of an automated process.

Controlling Payment Transfer Risks

Depository institutions, their primary regulators, and the Federal Reserve have focused increased attention on the credit risks inherent in large-dollar funds transfer systems. Credit risk — the risk that a party to a funds transfer will fail to settle the transfer — arises when a financial institution or a Federal Reserve Bank executes a payment order before it has received covering payment from its customer. Many depository institutions incur intraday, or "daylight," overdrafts in their accounts held at the Federal Reserve as a result of Fedwire funds transfers sent and payment for book-entry securities received. Similarly, institutions often permit their corporate customers to incur intraday overdrafts. (See the Daylight Overdrafts section in *The Commercial Banking Regulatory Handbook* for a full discussion of this topic.)

Evaluation of Credit Risks

Financial institutions should be able to monitor and control their overall position across all payment systems in which they participate. Institutions also should monitor the position of individual customers and control the amount of intraday credit extended to each customer within approved credit limits. Management should establish guidelines regarding payments that may exceed approved intraday and overnight overdraft limits, including the consideration that is given to projected incoming payments.

Intraday, or daylight, overdrafts are negative account positions during the business day. An institution should have the following procedures to safeguard against inappropriate daylight overdrafts:

- Established credit limits and regular internal credit reviews. In the absence of preauthorized limits, and institution should have a management approval process for daylight overdrafts. Authorization should be within the lending authority of approving officers; and

- Reporting and approval procedures for payments exceeding established credit limits to ensure that only officers with sufficient lending authority make approvals.

In addition to having controls for large-dollar funds and book-entry securities transfer activity, an institution should have controls for check learning, automated clearing house, currency operations, and other off-line payment activity that results in relatively large-value settlement obligations.

Operational and Communications Controls

An institution's internal controls should be designed to minimize the possibility of fraudulent transfers and losses due to errors and omissions resulting from a poor operating environment. Basic internal control routines must be in effect for any funds transfer operation to ensure that overall integrity is maintained. Controls are necessary for outgoing transactions, transfer system processing, and incoming credit transactions. An institution should have appropriate:

- Training of personnel engaged in the funds transfer process;

- Separation of duties for funds transfer personnel, including: origination, receipt, testing, approval, data entry, and release;

- Clearly defined security procedure over payment orders;

- Use of authentication and encryption devices;

- Monitoring of customers' intraday positions;

- Credit policy and effective procedures to control intraday and overnight overdrafts; and

- Provisions for maintaining compliance with regulatory reporting and review procedures

Communications Controls

Telecommunications systems used for EFTs can range from a simple connection between the institution and payments system (e.g., Fedwire) to terminal connections with customers that pass through the institution's funds transfer system directly to the payments systems. An institution should have a data security program that covers each interface and storage point of the system. The program may consist of personal identification numbers, passwords, or other identifying keys. Management should also consider encrypting data during transmission.

Retail Electronic Funds Transfer Systems

Automation has enabled banks to perform electronically many retail banking functions formerly handled manually by tellers, bookkeepers, data entry clerks, and other banking personnel. Examples of retail EFT systems include automated teller and loan processing machines, point-of-sale networks, debit and "smart" cards, and home and Internet banking. Accordingly, the need for physical banking facilities and related staff has been reduced.

EFT and related banking services also have brought access to, and control of, accounts closer to the consumer through use of widely distributed unmanned terminals and merchant facilities. EFT-related risk to a financial institution for individual customer transactions is generally low, because the transactions are usually for relatively small amounts. However, weaknesses in controls could lead to significant losses to or class action suits against a financial institution. (For discussion of the Electronic Fund Transfer Act, which is the primary federal law governing consumer rights in an EFT transaction involving a consumer asset account, see that section of *The Consumer Banking Regulatory Handbook*.)

Automated Teller Machines

Fraud, robbery, and malfunction are the major risks in an ATM environment. Although plastic cards and personal identification numbers (PINs) act as a deterrent to fraud, there is a risk that an unauthorized individual may obtain them. Customers even may be physically accosted while making withdrawals or deposits at ATM locations. Some institutions have decreased this risk by installing surveillance cameras and "access control devices."

Point-of-Sale Systems

As with other retail EFT systems, point-of-sale (POS) transactions are subject to risk of loss due to fraud, mistakes, and system malfunction. POS fraud is caused by stolen cards and PINs, counterfeit cards, and direct computer access. A POS system is also susceptible to errors such as debiting or crediting an account by too much or too little and entering unauthorized transactions. For the most part, POS systems usually deal with these risks by executing bank-merchant and bank-customer contracts that delineate each party's liabilities and responsibilities. Another risk inherent in POS systems is that of computer malfunction or downtime, and financial institutions offering POS services should provide for adequate records backup.

An institution's internal control guidelines for POS systems should address the following:

- Confidentiality and security of customer account information including protection of PINs;

- Maintenance of contracts between bank and merchants, customer and banks, and banks and network;

- Policies and procedures regarding credit and check authorization, floor limits, override, settlement, and balancing;

- Maintenance of transaction journals to provide an adequate audit trail;

- Generation and review of daily exception reports with provisions for backup and contingency planning; and

- Physical security surrounding POS terminal.

Debit and Smart Cards

Other funds transfer-related activities that use plastic card and PIN access are debit cards and smart cards. While not EFT systems by themselves, they may be used in conjunction with EFT systems. The cards may draw against available balances or lines of credit in related deposit accounts. They can be used for currency withdrawals at ATMs or for the direct purchase of goods or services from retailers using POS paper-based settlement systems.

A smart card contains a microchip that stores customer account profiles and credit line balances, as well as a record of transactions. When the customer uses the card to make a purchase or to withdraw cash, the terminal equipment deducts the amount from the balance remaining in the card's memory. Once the credit line in the card is exhausted, it will need replacement. Unlike POS systems, smart cards do not require on-line terminals.

Automated Clearing House (ACH)

While still primarily used for retail payments, an increasing number of large-dollar payments are made using automated clearing houses. The ACH is a nationwide electronic payments system used by a large number of depository institutions and corporations. ACH rules and regulations are established by the National Automated Clearing House Association (NACHA) and the local ACH associations, and are incorporated by reference in the Federal Reserve Banks' ACH operating circulars.

As with any funds transfer system, there are inherent risks in using the ACH, including error, credit risk, and fraud. An institution should maintain:

- Agreements covering delivery and settlement arrangements for its position as an originator or receiver of ACH transactions;

- Balancing procedures of ACH transactions processed;

- Monitoring procedures for the institution and customers' intraday positions;

- A credit policy and procedures to control intraday and overnight overdrafts, resulting from extensions of credit to ACH customers, to cover the value of credit transfers originated. (Note: The ACH is a value-dated mechanism in which institutions may originate transactions one or two days before the settlement date. Thus, the originating institution is exposed to risk from the time it submits ACH credit transfers to the ACH processor to the time its customer funds those transfers.);

- Controls for uncollected funds and the related credit policy for deposits created through ACH debit transactions. (Note: Although immediately available funds have been provided by the Federal Reserve for debit transactions deposited on a given day, the debits have not been posted to the payee's account and could be returned for insufficient funds or other reasons, such as a court order.);

- Exception reports, i.e., large item and new account reports;

- Control procedures for terminals through which additions, deletions, and other forms of maintenance could be made to customer databases; and

- All entries, return entries, and adjustment entries, transmitted to and received from the ACH for a period of six years after the date of the transmittal.

Internet Banking

Internet banking creates new challenges. Customer terminals and the delivery channels (e.g., public telephone networks and the Internet) are outside of the institution's control. The global reach of these systems increases the number of uncontrolled points of access to bank computer systems. These attributes introduce heightened security risks and emphasize the need to develop secure systems and procedures for operating in an uncontrolled environment.

An institution should evaluate the risks associated with existing or proposed PC banking programs, including all significant technology, legal, regulatory, and economic areas. Management should pay special attention to the following areas:

- Internal controls and audit trails;
- Authentication;
- Authorization;
- Compliance;
- Confidentiality;
- Information integrity;
- Capacity;
- Nonrepudiation;
- Outsourcing;
- Reliability; and
- Software updates.

Internet banking transactions should be subject to the same compliance laws and regulations that apply to traditional banking transactions. The application of those laws to Internet banking transactions raises questions, such as compliance with advertising and disclosure requirements. Financial institutions could risk regulatory enforcement and civil penalties for not complying with those laws and regulations.

To ensure a consistent regulatory policy for Internet banking, there are many issues that management should address, including:

- *Advertising* - creating appropriate triggers for existing advertising requirements for on-line interfaces;

- *Disclosures* - developing standards for using on-line disclosures, periodic statements, and notices rather than sending hard copies and determining whether downloadable documents and E-mail would be presented in a form the customer can retain; and

- *Document integrity* - developing standards for documents that the institution must deliver to the consumer to ensure that the consumer has received and downloaded the documents both accurately and entirely.

Nondeposit Investment Products

Marketing and selling securities and other uninsured instruments through either a closed network or the Internet potentially raises additional compliance issues. Regulators have stated that in delivering on-line services, institutions have not sufficiently separated banking from nonbanking activities. To protect themselves from liability, institutions must clearly distinguish insured from uninsured products and reinforce separate corporate identities. An insured institution's home screen or Internet home page, for example, must have the FDIC-Insured logo. However, institutions offering brokerage services must clarify to the customer that brokerage transactions are uninsured. At a minimum, at the transaction screen the institution should state that the transaction is uninsured. An inquiry requiring customer acknowledgment would be the better option.

> Institutions may subject themselves to substantial liability if their on-line services do not sufficiently distinguish insured products from uninsured products. To protect themselves, institutions should ensure that the system requires a customer to acknowledge that he is conducting an uninsured transaction.

Internal Controls for Retail EFTs

Regardless of the system employed, a financial institution should ensure it has in place adequate internal controls to minimize errors, discourage fraud, and provide an adequate audit trail. Recommended internal control guidelines include:

For all systems:

- Establishing proper customer identification (i.e., PINs) and maintaining confidentiality of customer account and PIN information;

- Issuing a receipt to the customer for each transaction;

- Installing a dependable file maintenance and retention system to trace transactions;

- Producing, reviewing, and maintaining exception reports to provide an audit trail;

- Requiring customers of each service to sign agreements that clearly define the responsibilities of the customer and the financial institution;

- Producing and forwarding periodic customers' statements so they can review transactions made during the period and detect unauthorized transfers, as required by Regulation E;

- Assuring adequate control of captured cards; and

- Protecting physical security surrounding ATM terminals.

For transfer and bill-paying systems:

- Allowing customer to pay bills or transfer funds only from their own accounts;

- Requiring preauthorization for specifically stated customer accounts; and

- Discouraging payments to third parties without written authorization.

The most critical element of EFT systems is the need for undisputed identification of the customer. Institutions should pay particular attention to the customer identification systems. The most common control is the issuance of a unique personal identification number that is used in conjunction with a plastic card or, for noncard systems, an account number. The American Bankers Association recommends that institutions use the following guidelines for protecting PIN numbers.

Storage

- Unissued PINs should never be stored before issuance. They should be calculated when issued and any temporary computer storage areas used in the calculation should be cleared immediately after use; and

- PINs should be encrypted on all files and databases.

Delivery

- PINs should not appear in printed form where they can be associated with customers' account numbers;

- Bank personnel should not have the capacity to retrieve or display customers' PINs via terminals;

- File access to PINs stored in databases should be restricted. Management should ensure that console logs or security reports are reviewed to determine any attempts to subvert the PIN security system; and

- PIN mailers should be processed and delivered with the same security accorded the delivery of bank cards to cardholders. (Note: A PIN should never be mailed to a customer together with the card.)

Usage

- The PIN should never be transmitted in unencrypted form;

- PIN systems should record the number of unsuccessful PIN entries and should restrict access to a customer's account after a few attempts (e.g., three); and

- If a customer forgets a PIN, the customer should select a new one other than having bank personnel retrieve the old one.

Control and Security

- Systems should be designed, tested, and controlled to preclude retrieval of stored PINs in any form;

- Application programs and other software containing formulas, algorithms, and data used to calculate PINs must be subject to the highest level of access for security purposes;

- Any data recording medium (e.g., magnetic tape and removable disks) used in the process of assigning, distributing, calculating, or encrypting PINs should be cleared immediately after use;

- Employees with access to PIN information should be subject to security clearance and covered by an adequate surety bond; and

- PIN systems should be designed so that PINs can be changed without reissuance of cards.

Insurance

Although computer-related employee defalcations are normally covered, financial institution blanket bond policies normally exclude certain types of electronic funds transfer activities from standard coverage. Management should consider separate coverage that is available for ATM, POS, and other EFT systems. An institution should consider self-insuring an EFT network only if the board of directors makes the decision and only after the board has been thoroughly briefed on the level of exposure.

End-User Computing and Networks

End-user computing (EUC) includes user-created or user-acquired systems that are maintained and operated outside the direct control of information resource (IR) professionals. The definition of an EUC system does not depend on particular hardware or software. The distinguishing factor is not what platform (i.e., personal computer, LAN mainframe) processes the system, but rather who is primarily responsible for the planning, development, security, operation, and maintenance of the system.

EUC systems theoretically do not include core business reporting or transaction processing systems. Systems that have either strategic or tactical importance to the business should be under the direct control of IR professionals.

While end-user computing systems provide certain advantages, there are increased risks to data integrity and data security, including:

- Difficulty in controlling access to the system;

- Lack of sophisticated software to assure security and data integrity;

- Insufficient capabilities to establish audit trails;

- Inadequate program testing and documentation; and

- Lack of segregation of duties.

The controls in an EUC environment should be no different from those implemented in a traditional mainframe information system environment. In this environment, local management and staff should assume responsibility for the information assets of the organization. Institutions that design reporting systems to fit their specific needs also have a competitive advantage.

Identify and Classify Existing EUC Applications and Data

As an initial step in assessing an EUC environment, management should inventory the nature and extent of existing EUC applications. This inventory should record hardware; software; software licenses and licensees; number of users; and the nature, purpose, volume, and usage of the applications. Management should assess also the sensitivity of applications and their data. Based on this inventory, management can make rational decisions regarding the importance to the institution of EUC systems and their ongoing viability in light of organizational goals and objectives.

Acquisition Criteria

Management also should establish appropriate standards and policies governing the acquisition and implementation of hardware and software and also support of end-user computing. Uncoordinated purchases could result in excessive costs, redundancy, incompatibility with other systems, and servicing complications. EUC acquisition policies may include:

- Feasibility studies at the user and management level;

- Development of a centralized purchased unit; and

- Corporatewide guidelines for user departments.

Security

Security in EUC environments refers to those controls that assure that the integrity and confidentiality of the system, information, and environment are maintained. While advances have been made regarding EUC technology, security remains a concern. Many times information that is tightly monitored and controlled in more complex computing environments (e.g., mainframe, minicomputer) is brought into the EUC environment for further user analysis (e.g., "screenscraping"). However, the ability to secure some EUC environments, such as personal computers, is hampered by the lack of control features in that environment. It is important that the same security controls and procedures applied on the larger-scale environment are applied to the EUC environment. The value of information assets to an institution remains the same, regardless of where the information resides. The absence of controls in this environment could affect management decisions made using information processed in this environment.

Management should consider the following:

- The application of security measures commensurate with the risk of loss and value of information;

- The defining of security administration roles, responsibilities, and procedures;

- User authentication and access control based on the assessment of risk to the organization; and

- Hardware security. While some EUC environments, such as LANs and file servers, may be quite sophisticated, personal computers present unique concerns.

Development

In the development of EUC applications, management should consider the same risks that are found in traditional processing environments. EUC development should address those controls intended to assure the integrity and reliability of the application or tool.

In many institutions, the advances of EUC technology and the explosion of EUC applications development have resulted in a large number of application systems that have become important to daily work processes. EUC applications may represent an increasingly significant investment. Management may rely on the accuracy and efficiency of these systems; accordingly, management should take care to ensure controlled development and maintenance of EUC application systems.

When developing EUC applications, management should consider the following areas:

- *Define requirements* - obtain a clear understanding of the business need driving the application or tool, the end-user's information requirements, and the expected improvements, or outcome, resulting from the successful implementation of the EUC application;

- *Evaluate alternatives* - compare information processing requirements against possible solutions; and

- *Build the application* - use programming tools to ensure that the resulting product operates as intended and yields consistent, reliable information.

    – Develop the detailed design or specifications for the application and assure controls are appropriate.

    – Review the design with other end-user applications.

    – Obtain approval from business management before constructing the application.

- Establish standards for developing EUC applications (naming, coding, screen design, report design).

- *Test the application* - validate that the EUC application meets the end-user processing and information requirements;

- *Implement the application* - execute the steps required to plan the application in a functional or operational mode; and

- *Maintain the application* - improve and upgrade the EUC application as the technology evolves. Application maintenance includes the controls that assure that the integrity of the application is maintained during and after a change is implemented.

Computer Usage

The use of EUC applications and assets refers to the daily operational tasks, such as storage management, maintenance, and support of the hardware and software. While the requirements of EUC environments are not as complex as large-scale mainframe or minicomputing environments, many of the objectives remain the same. The overriding consideration is the availability and reliability of the processing environment in order to promote integrity of the environment.

End-user systems are created for a specific need, whether to obtain data more rapidly or to present it in a more friendly manner. Even though a typical end-user system (i.e., database) is outside the day-to-day control of the IS function, it nonetheless should be controlled and monitored. Management should consider the following areas:

- *Monitor availability* - Define and prioritize tasks that require computer use for business operations. This is essential to maximizing the efficiency and effectiveness of the EUC environment;

- *Manage storage* - When containing data, media are as valuable as the data residing on them. Accordingly, media should be protected from unauthorized use, disclosure, modification, damage, and theft;

- *Perform backup and recovery* - The ability to save and restore critical or sensitive information is paramount to continuing business operations in the event of a disruption. An EUC environment, by nature, uses and produces information required for business decisions. The environment must support continuous availability of data in the event of a disruption;

- *Archive data* - As valuable disk space becomes scarce, information, though potentially valuable, may have to be removed from the computer and stored elsewhere until needed. Management should develop an archive strategy to plan, document, and execute an EUC environment's need for storing information over the long term;

- *Document procedures* - Accurate descriptions of hardware, software, and user procedures should be kept for use in the department. Documentation helps to assure consistency of use among users and to prevent undue reliance on key individuals;

- *Control changes and upgrades* - Changes to hardware and software in terms of version upgrades, program modifications, and hardware modifications should be controlled to prevent unauthorized computer activity. Management should also ensure that changes to a system are documented and evaluated for potential impact on the processing environment;

- *Conform to software licenses* - Because an EUC system is prone to use packaged software solutions (i.e., spreadsheets, databases, word processors), users must be aware of, and comply with, applicable copyrights and licensing issues; and

- *Scan for viruses* - The end-user should develop and follow a systematic approach to scanning for viruses to avoid virus-induced damage to computer resources.

Communications

The most dramatic changes in EUC have occurred in the area of communications. Communications refers to user-controlled communications facilities, such as modems, PC to PC transmissions, PC to mainframe or midrange transmissions, and end-user controlled LANs.

Communications systems provide an access path to many corporate assets; therefore, management should address security and control. Communications systems can be attacked by programs, such as viruses, which if undetected or unchecked could significantly affect the entire processing community. Communications systems also can be attacked by hackers. Accordingly, it is the responsibility of all end-users to ensure that the use of communications facilities is properly monitored and controlled.

When evaluating communications, management should consider the following areas:

- *Identify existing communications capabilities* - It is important to understand the nature and extent of EUC Communications because such situations may provide an open window into the larger institution community. Accordingly, management should assure that appropriate security and control mechanisims are in place;

- *Assess exposures* - Assessing exposure involves understanding the nature and purpose of the communications facility and its importance. Critical processing facilities require a greater degree of control;

- *Approve requests for communications* - The approval process involves the understanding and evaluation of security and control features before the implementation of a communications facility or device. Management should evaluate all applications that involve communications, especially with external organizations; and

- *Document procedures and monitor the environment* - Documenting procedures and monitoring the environment involve the daily management processes for the security and control of communications facilities.

Document Imaging

Imaging systems permit institutions to streamline workflow processes, reduce storage and retrieval costs, and improve customer service by automating customer files and correspondence. They are used to capture, index, store, and retrieve electronic images of paper documents. These systems present new concerns and challenges for the board of directors, who must ensure that the risks are addressed by the institution's management.

Control and Security Risk Areas

Replacing paper documents with electronic images can have a significant impact on the way that an institution does business. Many of the traditional audit and security controls for paper-based systems may be reduced or absent in electronic document workflow. An institution must develop new controls and incorporate them into the automated process to ensure that information in image files cannot be altered, erased, or lost.

References

Process and Control Guidelines for Wholesale Funds Transfer Systems, Bank Administration Institute (BAI); and

Information Systems Examination Handbook, 2 vols., 1996 Edition, Federal Financial Institutions Examination Council (FFIEC).

VII. The Year 2000

Introduction and Purpose 110

External Risk Issues 118

Operational Issues 119

Introduction and Purpose

The Year 2000 poses serious challenges to the banking industry. The Year 2000 problem — or the inability of computers to recognize dates beyond 1999 — could potentially cause national and worldwide computer systems to shut down or make major mistakes at the turn of the century. The federal bank regulators thus have undertaken a major effort to mitigate the effect of the Year 2000 problem on the safety and soundness of banks and savings and loans.

Background

> The year 2000 problem—or the inability of computers to recognize dates beyond 1999 – could potentially cause national and worldwide computer systems to shut down or make mistakes at the turn of the century.

Most computer systems — particularly mainframes — cannot distinguish the year 1900 from the year 2000. Computer operating systems typically use a six-digit date field (YYMMDD), which represents, for example, December 31, 1999, as 991231. As a space-saving mechanism, computer programmers dropped the first two numbers of the year, abbreviating 1999 as 99. Because of this abbreviation, computer systems cannot recognize a date past year-end 1999. Instead, systems will interpret January 1, 2000, as January 1, 1900; January 1, 2001 as January 1, 1901, and so on.

Y2K Timeline

In May 1997, the FFIEC issued an Interagency Statement emphasizing the importance of financial institutions taking steps to meet the Year 2000 problem ("Y2K"). The bank regulatory agencies intend to examine each financial institution's Y2K conversion efforts by mid-1998. Institutions should meet the following key target dates:

- Identify critical computer functions (September 30, 1997 was the deadline date); and

- Revise code and upgrade hardware by December 31, 1998. Regulators will assess mission-critical applications to assure that programming changes are largely completed and that testing is well under way by this date.

Federal regulators intend to work closely with institutions facing unusual difficulties to assure that these institutions focus on problem areas and devote adequate attention to achieving Y2K solutions.

FRB Supervisory Letter on Y2K

In November 1997, the Federal Reserve issued a supervisory letter indicating that organizations whose computer systems are unprepared to recognize the turn of the century date change could face a reduction of their CAMELS or equivalent rating, rejection of applications for mergers or acquisitions, or enforcement actions including civil penalties. The letter also emphasizes the importance of minimizing external risk, alerts branches or agencies of foreign banks to examination criteria, and emphasizes consumer issues, and outlines postexamination supervisory procedures.

External Risk

The term "external risk" refers to the risk that another party's failure to deal with the Y2K issue could affect a banking organization. In particular, corporate borrowers that depend on computer systems that could be adversely affected by the Y2K problems might face difficulties that jeopardize their ability to repay loans. The Federal Reserve advises institutions to incorporate Y2K readiness in their underwriting and loan review standards and consider including Y2K compliance provisions in loan agreements to minimize their exposure to external risks.

Examination of Foreign Branches and Agencies

The Board is examining foreign branches' and agencies' progress in solving their Y2K problems. The Federal Reserve Bank conducting an examination may discuss deficiencies with senior management of the parent foreign bank directly depending on the extent of the problems uncovered. If necessary, the Board will bring enforcement actions using the same criteria as for U.S. organizations.

The Board also is attempting to ensure that foreign banks that interact electronically with the U.S. are ready for the turn of the century.

Consumer Protections

The Board is particularly concerned with institutions' ability to provide uninterrupted services to their customers and comply with all consumer-protection laws and rules. Although organizations usually integrate compliance with these laws into their overall information systems, examiners must incorporate consumer compliance issues into their workpapers. Any problems with consumer-protection issues will be included in the examiner's comments and considered when the FRB determines the need to bring an enforcement action.

Supervisory Follow-Up Procedures

If Board examiners find an institution's Y2K planning, project management, and assessment programs unsatisfactory, they will require the institution to submit a written plan for Y2K compliance to their Federal Reserve Bank. The plan must describe management's efforts to address all deficiencies related to the Y2K issue and set an acceptable compliance schedule. Institutions with unsatisfactory Y2K compliance will also have to submit monthly progress reports. If the plan and the progress reports indicate that the institution will have difficulties fixing its Y2K problems, the Federal Reserve Bank will recommend additional suitable enforcement action. If serious problems exist the FRB may impose a written agreement, a cease-and-desist order, or civil money penalties.

Board of Directors' Responsibilities

In December 1997, the FFIEC issued additional safety and soundness guidelines that outline the board of directors' responsibilities. The board should ensure that senior management is taking an enterprisewide approach to address Y2K problems and providing sufficient resources to resolve these problems. Regulators expect that an institution's Y2K problem program will:

- Include sufficient coordination between business units and the institution's operational risk management functions as conversion programs are executed; determine a vendor's progress in resolving Y2K problems for their information processing software or products;

- Determine the readiness of the institution's systems for testing;

- Involve parties throughout the institution in the coordination of readiness efforts and the development of contingency plans;

- Require comprehensive testing of applications with all internal and external systems that share information. Senior management will monitor this testing for all mission-critical systems; and

- Develop processes to identify, assess, and control the potential Y2K credit risk in their lending and investment portfolios.

The board must, at a minimum, require quarterly status reports from management that detail the organization's progress in addressing Y2K issues. The board should receive immediate notice if the project fails to meet critical benchmarks. Reports to the board should include, but not necessarily be limited to, updates concerning:

- Overall progress of the Y2K project, including any new efforts initiated since the last report;

- Progress plotted against the institution's Y2K project plan, including comparisons against performance benchmarks;

- Status of efforts by key vendors, business partners, counter parties, and major loan customers to address Y2K issues, including any weaknesses discovered and critical date decisions;

- Results of internal and external testing of information procession applications, databases, and systems; and

- Contingency planning efforts that outline alternative courses of action in the event existing internal systems or external systems provided by vendors will not be ready for Y2K.

Institutions renovating their own mission-critical applications should tailor their reports to the complexity of the applications and provide information that:

- Identifies the total number of applications inventoried during the assessment phase and details the number of mission-critical applications in each stage of the five-step project management process outlined below in *Management Guidelines*;

- Informs the board about the progress being made to complete the renovation, testing, and implementation of mission-critical applications;

- Identifies the number of mission-critical applications grouped by the intended resolution strategy; and

- Summarizes the results of internal and external testing.

Board minutes should reflect any material action taken by the Board to address Y2K issues or concerns. Board reporting should be available for review by examiners during on-site and off-site supervisory activities.

Project Planning and Management

The Y2K problem requires extensive project planning to ensure proper allocations of resources and management accountability. Institutions should adopt an enterprisewide plan containing clearly defined objectives and deadlines. The plan should include:

- The tasks to be accomplished throughout the term of the project;

- The resource requirements and individuals assigned responsibility for various phases of the project;

- The specific dates for completion of key elements of the project; and

- The strategy for responding to inquiries from customers and business partners regarding the institution's Y2K readiness.

Senior management should actively manage resources to ensure their Y2K project remains on schedule and implement processes that monitor vendors, business partners, counter parties, and major loan customers' Y2K efforts. Institutions must exercise appropriate due diligence in their budget planning to ensure that they have sufficient financial and human resources to complete their Y2K plans in a timely manner.

Assessment Questionnaire

Regulators will utilize a questionnaire issued by the FFIEC in their initial assessment of an institution's Y2K planning efforts. The questionnaire is designed to capture macro-level information on Y2K preparations from financial institutions and their information systems vendors. Regulators will be looking for an established, comprehensive plan of action taking into account:

- Capability of information processing and delivery systems to handle Y2K processing;

- Identification and prioritization of primary systems at risk;

- Adequate resource allocation (i.e., hardware, people, dollars);

- Monitoring and sponsorship by management; and

- Timeliness.

The regulatory agencies will use the results of this assessment to prioritize on-site examinations and will target first those institutions that have not actively begun a Y2K conversion program.

On-Site Examination Procedures

Regulators will utilize the following procedures in their examination of a financial institution's conversion efforts. The examination's objectives are to:

- Determine whether the organization has an effective plan for identifying, renovating, testing, and implementing solutions for Y2K processing;

- Assess the effect of Y2K efforts on the organization's strategic and operating plans;

- Determine whether the organization has effectively coordinated Y2K processing capabilities with its customers, vendors, and payment system partners;

- Assess the soundness of internal controls for the Y2K process; and

- Identify whether further corrective action may be necessary to assure an appropriate level of attention to Y2K processing capabilities.

Management Guidelines

In order to assist a financial institution in achieving Y2K compliance, the FFIEC outlines in the examination procedures five management phases necessary to complete a computer conversion program:

- Awareness;
- Assessment;
- Renovation;
- Validation; and
- Implementation.

In addition, the FFIEC identifies several operational and external risk issues that a Y2K conversion plan should consider.

Awareness

Define the Y2K problem and establish a management team that encompasses in-house systems, service bureaus for systems that are outsourced, vendors, auditors, customers, and suppliers (including correspondents). Regulators expect senior management to establish project target dates and to monitor the project's progress. Regulators will audit minutes from board of directors and committee meetings documenting Y2K discussions.

Assessment

Assess the size and complexity of the problem and detail the magnitude of the effort necessary to address Y2K issues. Identify all hardware, software, networks, automated teller machines, other various processing platforms, and customer and vendor interdependencies affected by the Y2K date change. The assessment must go beyond information systems and include environmental systems that are dependent on embedded microchips, such as security systems, elevators, and vaults.

Management also must evaluate the Y2K effect on other strategic business initiatives. The assessment should consider the potential effect that mergers and acquisitions, major system development, corporate alliances, and system interdependencies will have on existing systems and/or the potential Y2K issues that may arise from acquired systems.

Renovation

This phase includes code enhancements, hardware and software upgrades, system replacements, vendor certification, and other associated changes. Management should prioritize work based on information gathered during the assessment phase. For institutions relying on outside servicers or third-party software providers, ongoing discussions and monitoring of vendor progress are necessary.

Validation

Testing is critical throughout the Y2K process. Management should test incremental changes to hardware and software components. All changes should be accepted by internal and external users. Management should establish controls to assure the effective and timely completion of all hardware and software testing prior to final implementation. Ongoing discussions with vendors concerning the success of their validation efforts is also necessary.

Implementation

Systems should be certified as Y2K compliant and be accepted by business users. Any potentially noncompliant mission-critical system should be brought to the attention of executive management immediately for resolution. In addition, this phase must assure that any new systems or subsequent changes to verified systems meet Y2K requirements.

Clarification of the Certification Requirements

Certification alone does not provide adequate assurances that a product will operate properly in the unique environments of multiuser financial institutions. Only a comprehensive test of all internal and external systems and system interdependencies will ensure that they will function properly together. Therefore, formal certification is not required. Institutions should communicate with their vendors and conduct due diligence inquiries concerning Y2K readiness and implement their own internal testing or verification processes pertaining to these vendor services and products to ensure that their systems and data function properly together. They should monitor closely their vendor's progress in meeting target deadlines. The vendor's plan should allow adequate time for user testing in a Y2K environment. Institutions should address the following topics with vendors:

- Dates that products will be Y2K ready or available for testing;

- Products that will not be Y2K ready, or will no longer be supported;

- Methods used to renovate the product or system;

- The pivot year, if the windowing method is used;

- Any efforts that require coordination between the institution, its vendor, and any other parties involved in external testing; and

- Vendor guidance on user testing of products.

Institutions should develop contingency plans for all vendors that service mission-critical applications and establish a trigger date for implementing alternative solutions should the vendor not complete its conversion efforts on time. Contingency plans should be reviewed at least quarterly and adjusted to reflect current circumstances.

Management should have a thorough understanding of the complex interrelationships between its systems and vendors' systems to establish relevant trigger dates. Institutions should consider the time needed to convert the existing system to one that is ready for the Y2K, the staff training time needed to implement an alternative system, and the availability of alternative systems. If the institution's or its vendor's Y2K conversions will not be completed on time, management should be ready to implement its contingency plans. For complex applications, management may have to begin implementation of the contingency plan while continuing to work on the desired solution.

The contingency plan should identify how the institution will transition to an alternate system or an external vendor for in-house developed applications. These plans should also identify alternative suppliers and outline migration plans for institutions that rely on vendors. Time frames for Y2K contingency plans should be consistent with the time frames discussed above in **Y2K Timeline**. This timeline establishes December 31, 1998, as the date that institutions should have completed programming changes and have testing well under way for mission-critical systems.

Industry Coordination

The FFIEC member agencies strongly encourage institutions and their trade organizations to cooperate in addressing issues pertaining to the Y2K. Effective cooperation can help reduce costs. Institutions can share ideas, influence vendors, develop best management practices, and maintain their competitiveness with other industries.

External Risk Issues

Management should consider the following external risks:

- *Reliance on Vendors*. Management should evaluate vendor plans and actively monitor project milestones. Institutions should determine if vendor contract terms can be revised explicitly to include Y2K covenants. Management also should be aware of their institution's vulnerability if the vendor cannot meet contractual obligations and consider alternate service or software providers if vendor solutions or time frames are inadequate.

- *Data Exchange*. Large volumes of date-sensitive data are transferred electronically between financial institutions, their customers, and their regulators. Institutions will need to know how methods of data exchange differ among financial institutions, across vendors, and between other institutions.

  The project plan should include testing and verification, as appropriate, of data exchanges with clearing associations, governmental entities, customers, and international financial institutions.

- *Corporate Customers*. Corporate customers, who have not considered Y2K issues, may experience a disruption in business, resulting in potentially significant financial difficulties that could affect their creditworthiness. Institutions should periodically assess large corporate customer Y2K efforts and consider writing Y2K compliance into their loan documentation. Loan and credit review officers should consider in their credit analysis of large corporate customers whether the borrower's Y2K conversion efforts are sufficient to avoid significant disruptions to operations.

Operational Issues

Management should consider the following operational issues:

- *Replacement v. Repair.* In some instances, replacing equipment may prove less expensive than extensive repairs;

- *Mergers and Acquisitions.* Acquisition strategies should include the institution's Y2K assessment to the extent possible;

- *Contracts.* Legal issues may arise from the lack of specificity in contract terms dealing with Y2K issues. Banks may wish to modify vendor contracts to detail vendor responsibilities in addressing Y2K issues. Current and future purchases should require Y2K certification. If contract changes or modification are refused, then the institution should consider replacing the service or product; and

- *September 9, 1999 / Leap Year (February 29, 2000).* All Y2K plans should address the September 9, 1999, and leap year — February 29, 2000 — issues. The September date (9/9/99) poses a potential problem because many computer programs interpret 9999 as a command to cease certain functions. The year 2000 is a leap year; however, many computer programs are not written to reflect February 29, 2000. Management should review all date and calculation routines to ensure that September 9, 1999, and leap year calculations are Y2K certified.

VIII. Financial Institutions Ratings Systems

Introduction 122

The Five-Point Scale 122

The Elements of the Composite Ratings 125

Uniform Financial Institutions Rating System – CAMELS 125

CAMELS Overview 126

CAMELS — The FDICIA Connection 136

Uniform Interagency Trust Rating System 137

Ratings of Foreign Banking Organizations 146

The Bank Holding Company Rating System – BOPEC 151

The Consumer Compliance Rating System 167

The Uniform Interagency Rating System for Data Processing Organizations 170

The Off-Site Rating Systems — SEER and NBSS 174

Introduction

The federal financial institution regulators have established uniform systems of evaluating the condition of their supervised institutions. Their evaluations, usually expressed as a numerical composite rating, increasingly reflect the regulators' assessment of the institution's risk management abilities.

In this portion of the *Handbook* we will discuss these rating systems:

- The Uniform Financial Institutions Rating System (UFIRS), better known as the CAMELS system, which evaluates the safety and soundness of institutions insured through either of the two FDIC insurance funds;

- The Uniform Interagency Trust Rating System, or UITRS, which evaluates the condition of trust departments and trust companies;

- The Federal Reserve's ROCA and SOSA systems under which it evaluates the condition of U.S. offices of foreign banks;

- The Federal Reserve's BOPEC system under which the Federal Reserve evaluates the condition of bank holding companies;

- The Consumer Compliance Rating system under which the four federal banking agencies rate institutions' compliance with consumer laws and regulations;

- The Uniform Interagency Rating System for Data Processing Organizations; and

- The off-site ratings used by the Federal Reserve, FDIC, and Comptroller of the Currency.

Regulators use a unique four-point system developed by the FFIEC in considering an institution's Community Reinvestment (CRA) performance. Because the CRA rating does not incorporate a risk management component, we have not included a discussion of it in this book. A discussion of CRA compliance appears in *The Consumer Banking Regulatory Handbook*.

The Five-Point Scale

In each of the systems, the regulators have developed an overall rating on a five-point scale. For all systems, except the SOSA, which applies to foreign bank branches and agencies, the ratings are 1 through 5. The SOSA, because it works in tandem with the numerically oriented ROCA rating, uses the letters A through E.

Although the entities evaluated under these systems are very different, the meaning of a composite rating under any of the systems is very similar. Whether it is a savings and loan, a trust department, an agency of a foreign bank, a multibank holding company, the consumer operations of an institution, a data processing center, or any other rated entity or activity, the regulators' description of the ratings remain remarkably constant. The rating scale of one through five (or A through E) expresses an ascending order of supervisory concern. Thus, "1" (or "A") represents the highest rating and, consequently, the lowest level of supervisory concern; while "5" (or "E") represents the lowest, most critically deficient level of performance and, therefore, the highest degree of supervisory concern.

We have developed this explanation of the five-point scale from a combination of the regulatory texts for examiners. With the exception of a few changes in wording, such as the UITRS emphasis on trust activities and compliance with fiduciary responsibilities, the five-point scales in use for the ratings systems bear a strong similarity to each other.

Composite 1

This group represents the institutions that are superior in all respects and generally have components rated 1 or 2. Any weaknesses are minor in nature and can be handled in a routine manner. These institutions are more capable of withstanding the vagaries of business conditions and are resistant to outside influences such as economic instability in their trade area. They are in a strong compliance position. As a result, these financial institutions exhibit strong performance and risk management practices relative to their size, complexity, and risk profile, and give no cause for supervisory concern.

Composite 2

An institution in this group is fundamentally sound. To receive a 2 rating, generally, no component rating should be more severe than 3. Only moderate weaknesses are present and are well within the board of directors' and management's capabilities and willingness to correct. A composite 2-rated institution is stable and capable of withstanding business fluctuations. It is in substantial compliance with laws and regulations. Overall risk management practices are satisfactory relative to the institution's size, complexity, and risk profile. There are no material supervisory concerns and, as a result, the supervisory response is informal and limited. Features subject to criticism may include isolated instances of noncompliance with laws, regulations, or management-prescribed policies and procedures, but corrective action without loss to customers is assured.

> Regulators have made a good rating more valuable. As of January 15, 1997, all banks with CAMELS ratings of 1 or 2 and with less than $250 million in assets will be examined on 18-month cycles rather than 12-month cycles. Banks with a rating of 1 or 2 are entitled to quick processing on some applications.

Composite 3

An institution in this group exhibits some degree of supervisory concern in one or more of the component areas. A composite 3-rated financial institution exhibits a combination of weaknesses that may range from moderate to severe; however, the magnitude of the deficiencies generally will not cause a component to be rated more severely than 4. Management may lack the ability or willingness to address weaknesses effectively within an appropriate time. An institution in this group generally is less capable of withstanding business fluctuations and is more vulnerable to outside influences than those institutions rated a composite 1 or 2. Additionally, the institution may be in significant noncompliance with laws and regulations. A 3-rated institution requires more than normal supervision, which may include formal or informal enforcement actions. Failure appears unlikely, however, given the overall strength and financial capacity of these institutions.

The supervisory response is ordinarily limited to follow-up on correction of features criticized in an examination.

Composite 4

An institution in this group generally exhibits unsafe and unsound practices or conditions. There are serious financial or managerial deficiencies resulting in unsatisfactory performance. The problems range from severe to critically deficient, and the board of directors or management are not satisfactorily addressing or resolving them. An institution in this group generally is not capable of withstanding business fluctuations. Examiners may also find significant noncompliance with laws and regulations. Risk management practices are generally unacceptable relative to the institution's size, complexity, and risk profile.

Unless management or the regulator or both take effective action to correct the criticized conditions, the 4-rated institution could reasonably develop into a situation that could impair future viability, constitute a threat to the interests of depositors or beneficiaries, or pose a risk to the deposit insurance fund. Close supervisory attention is required, which means, in most cases, formal enforcement action is necessary to address the problems. Failure is a distinct possibility if the problems and weaknesses are not satisfactorily addressed and resolved.

Composite 5

This category is reserved for institutions with an extremely high immediate or near-term probability of failure. The volume and severity of weaknesses or unsafe and unsound conditions are so critical as to require urgent aid from stockholders or other public or private sources of financial assistance. Risk management practices are inadequate relative to the institution's size, complexity, and risk profile. The 5-rated institution has a weak compliance position. Its management may have a flagrant disregard for the law.

The Elements of the Composite Ratings

Examiners review several aspects of an institution's operations and activities during the course of their on-site work. They rate each of those activities on a five-point scale and determine a composite rating after consideration of the ratings for the several elements.

Thus,

- 1 = Strong, excellent, or superior;
- 2 = Satisfactory;
- 3 = Fair;
- 4 = Marginal or weak; and
- 5 = Unsatisfactory or hazardous.

Beginning in the fall of 1996, FDIC examiners disclosed ratings for all composites and components of the CAMELS rating system. As of January 1, 1997, other federal bank regulators disclose the composite and component ratings in their CAMELS ratings.

Uniform Financial Institutions Rating System — CAMELS

The Federal Financial Institutions Examination Council (FFIEC) recommended the Uniform Financial Institutions Rating System to its members in 1978. In December 1996, the FFIEC amended the rating system to include additional evaluation factors. While the official name is the Uniform Financial Institutions Ratings System, most regulators, bankers, and others familiar with it refer to it by the acronym "CAMEL" or "CAMELS." (We describe the source of the acronym in the Performance Evaluation section below.) The Federal Reserve, FDIC, and Comptroller of the Currency adopted the uniform system as the CAMEL (now CAMELS) rating system upon its proposal by the FFIEC. The Federal Home Loan Bank Board followed a nearly identical system but used the MACRO acronym. In 1993, after the Office of

Thrift Supervision replaced the Federal Home Loan Bank Board, the OTS shifted as well to the CAMELS system of the other three bank regulators.

The term "financial institution," with respect to the rating system refers to certain institutions whose primary federal supervisory agencies are represented on the Federal Financial Institutions Examination Council. They include federally supervised commercial banks, savings and loan associations, mutual savings banks, and credit unions. For purposes of this *Handbook*, we use the term to include only banks and thrift institutions, but not credit unions because of their unique corporate and tax structure.

The rating system provides a general framework for evaluating and assimilating all significant financial, operational, and compliance factors in order to assign a summary or composite supervisory rating to each federally regulated financial institution. The purpose of the rating system is to reflect in a comprehensive and uniform fashion an institution's financial condition, compliance with laws and regulations, sensitivity to market risk, and overall operating soundness. In addition to serving as a useful tool for summarizing the condition of individual institutions, the rating framework also assists the public and Congress in assessing the aggregate strength and soundness of the financial industry.

To some degree, each type of financial institution poses its own set of supervisory issues and concerns. The uniform rating system is predicated upon certain features and functions, including qualitative and quantitative factors, common to all categories of institutions.

CAMELS Overview

Regulators assign each financial institution a uniform composite rating reflecting an evaluation of financial and operational standards, criteria, and principles. In assigning a composite rating, regulators consider a variety of factors. In general, these factors include:

- The adequacy of the capital base, net worth, and reserves for supporting present operations and future growth plans;

- The quality of loans, investments, and other assets;

- The ability of management to identify, measure, monitor, and control market risks;

- The ability to generate earnings to maintain public confidence, cover losses, and provide adequate security and return to depositors;

- The ability to manage liquidity and funding;

- The ability to meet the community's legitimate needs for financial services and cover all maturing deposit obligations; and

- The ability of management to properly administer all aspects of the financial business and plan for future needs and changing circumstances.

The assessment of management and administration includes the quality of internal controls, operating procedures, and all lending, investment, and operating policies; the compliance with relevant laws and regulations; and the involvement of the directors, shareholders, and officials. In general, the regulators' assignment of a composite rating may incorporate any other factors that bear significantly on the overall condition and soundness of the financial institution.

Notwithstanding their use of common summary ratings, regulators apply specific performance benchmarks, standards, and principles in order to recognize existing structural, operational, and regulatory distinctions among different types of financial institutions. Thus, a regulator evaluates each financial institution upon criteria relating to its particular industry. The assignment of a uniform composite rating helps to direct uniform and consistent supervisory attention in a way that does not depend solely upon the nature of an institution's charter or business, or the identity of its primary federal regulator.

The primary purpose of the uniform rating system is to help identify those institutions whose financial, operating, risk management, or compliance weaknesses require special supervisory attention or warrant a higher than normal degree of supervisory concern. These institutions are, depending upon degree of risk and supervisory concern, rated composite "4" or "5." This group of institutions carries a relatively high possibility of failure or insolvency generally and can be characterized by unsafe, unsound, or other seriously unsatisfactory conditions.

The rating system also identifies institutions that have some combination of financial or compliance difficulties — the 3-rated institutions. While posing little or no threat to financial viability under present circumstances, these institutions do warrant more than normal supervisory concern. The delineation of this category assists supervisory authorities in separating the most serious and critical problem institutions, whose viability may be in question, from those institutions whose financial or compliance deficiencies may require a specific supervisory response but do not constitute a significant risk of failure, insolvency, or bankruptcy.

Performance Evaluation

The rating system is based upon an evaluation of six critical dimensions of a financial institution's operations that reflect in a comprehensive fashion an institution's financial condition, compliance with banking regulations and statutes, and overall operating soundness. The regulators evaluate these specific dimensions.

- Capital adequacy;
- Asset quality;
- Management and administration;
- Earnings;
- Liquidity; and
- Sensitivity to market risk.

The CAMELS acronym comes from the first letter of each of the six dimensions.

Regulators rate each of these dimensions on a scale of one through five in descending order of performance quality. Thus, 1 represents the highest and 5 the lowest (and most critically deficient) level of operating performance. In assigning performance ratings, regulators use these gradations:

Rating No. 1 — indicates strong performance and risk management practices. It is the highest rating and indicates performance that is significantly higher than average.

Rating No. 2 — reflects satisfactory performance and risk management practices. It reflects performance that is average or above; it includes performance that adequately provides for the safe and sound operation of the bank.

Rating No. 3 — represents performance and risk management practices that are flawed to some degree. It indicates only fair performance — performance that is neither satisfactory nor marginal but is of below average quality.

Rating No. 4 — represents marginal performance and risk management practices which are significantly below average. If left unchecked, marginal performance might evolve into weaknesses or conditions that could threaten the viability of the institution.

Rating No. 5 — represents unsatisfactory performance and risk management practices. It is the lowest rating and indicates performance that is critically deficient and in need of immediate remedial attention. This performance by itself, or in combination with other weaknesses, could threaten the viability of the institution.

Capital Adequacy

Regulators rate capital 1 through 5 in relation to:

- The level and quality of capital, and the ability of management to address emerging needs for additional capital;

- The nature, trend, and volume of problem assets, and the adequacy of allowances for loan and lease losses and other valuation reserves;

- Balance sheet composition, including the nature and amount of intangible assets, market risk, concentration risk, and risks associated with nontraditional activities;

- Risk exposure represented by off-balance sheet activities; and

- The financial institution's growth experience, plans, and prospects.

In addition, an examiner may consider a financial institution's capital ratios relative to its peer group, its earnings retention, and its access to capital markets or other appropriate sources of financial assistance.

A financial institution rated 1 or 2 has adequate capital relative to the institution's risk profile, although a 1-rated institution's capital ratios will generally exceed those of a 2-rated institution. Examiners will assign a 3 rating to an institution's capital position when they determine that there is an adverse relationship of the capital structure to risk assets; marginal and low-quality assets; or its business prospects, plans, or experience. Institutions rated 4 and 5 are clearly inadequately capitalized, the latter group representing a situation of such gravity as to threaten viability and solvency.

A 5 rating also denotes an institution that requires urgent assistance from shareholders or other external sources of financial support.

Asset Quality

Examiners rate asset quality 1 through 5 in relation to:

- Adequacy of underwriting standards and appropriateness of risk identification practices;

- Level, distribution, severity, and trend of problem, nonaccrual, restructured, delinquent, and nonperforming assets for both on- and off-balance sheet transactions;

- Credit risk arising from or reduced by off-balance sheet transactions, such as unfunded commitments, credit derivatives, commercial and standby letters of credit, and lines of credit;

- Adequacy of valuation reserves;

- Adequacy of internal controls and management information systems;

- Diversification and quality of loan and investment portfolios; and

- Demonstrated ability to administer and collect problem credits.

Adequate valuation reserves and a proven capacity to police and collect problem credits mitigate to some degree the weaknesses in a given level of classified assets. In evaluating asset quality, examiners also consider any undue degree of concentration of credits or investments, the nature and volume of special mention classifications, lending policies, and the adequacy of credit administration procedures.

Asset quality ratings of 1 and 2 represent situations involving a minimal level of supervisory concern, although the level and severity of classifications of the latter generally exceed those of the former. Both ratings represent sound portfolios and modest risk exposure in relation to capital protection and management's abilities. A 3 asset rating indicates a situation involving an appreciable degree of concern, especially to the extent that current adverse trends suggest potential future problems. Trends may be stable or indicate deterioration in asset quality or increased risk exposure. Generally, a 3 rating shows a need to improve both credit administration and risk management practices. Ratings 4 and 5 represent increasingly more severe asset problems; rating 5, in particular, represents an imminent threat to bank viability through the corrosive effect of asset problems on the level of capital support.

Management and Administration

Management's performance must be evaluated against virtually all factors necessary to operate the bank within accepted banking practices and in a safe and sound manner. Thus, examiners will rate management 1 through 5 with respect to:

- Accuracy, timeliness, and effectiveness of management information and risk monitoring systems appropriate to the institution's size, complexity, and risk profile;

- Ability to plan for and respond to risks arising from changing business conditions or the initiation of new products;

- Adequacy of audits and internal controls to promote effective operations, reliable financial and regulatory reporting, and safeguard assets;

- Compliance with banking regulations and statutes;

- Adequacy of and compliance with internal policies;

- Responsiveness to recommendations from auditors and supervisory authorities;

- Management depth and succession;

- Reasonableness of compensation and tendencies toward self-dealing;

- Demonstrated willingness to serve the legitimate banking needs of the community; and

- Overall performance of the institution and its risk profile.

A 1 rating indicates a management that is fully effective with respect to almost all factors and exhibits a responsiveness and ability to cope successfully with existing and foreseeable problems that may arise in the conduct of the bank's affairs. Strong risk management practices exist relative to the institution's size, complexity, and risk profile. A 2 rating reflects some deficiencies but generally indicates a satisfactory record of performance and risk management practices relative to the institution's size, complexity, and risk profile.

A 3 rating indicates management and board performance in need of improvement or risk management practices that are less satisfactory given the nature of the institution's activities. The 3-rated institution usually has modestly talented management when above average abilities are called for, or management is distinctly below average for the type, size, or condition of the bank that it operates. Thus, its responsiveness or ability to correct less than satisfactory conditions may be lacking. The 4 rating indicates management that is generally inferior in ability compared to the responsibilities with which it is charged. Replacing or strengthening management or the board may be necessary. A rating of 5 indicates critically deficient management and board performance or risk management practices. In these cases, problems result-

> Regulators evaluate management on its own merits and also in conjunction with the overall condition of the institution. The result is that all deficiencies reflect on management and management will almost always receive a rating that is close to the institution's rating for capital or asset quality. Management that would be rated a 1 in a strong institution will be rated a 2 or 3 in one with a 3 rating for asset quality, for instance.

ing from management weakness threaten the continued viability of the institution. Management must be strengthened or replaced before the institution can return to a sound condition.

Earnings

Examiners rate earnings 1 through 5 with respect to:

- Ability to cover losses and provide for adequate capital through retained earnings;

- Level of earnings, including trends and stability;

- Quality, composition, and source of earnings;

- Adequacy of budgeting systems, forecasting processes, and management information systems in general;

- Adequacy of allowances for loan and lease losses and other valuation allowance accounts;

- Earnings exposure to market risk such as interest rate, foreign exchange, and price risks;

- Operational expenses; and

- Peer group comparisons.

Regulators also consider the interrelationships that exist between the dividend payout ratio, the rate of growth of retained earnings, and the adequacy of bank capital. A dividend payout rate that is sufficiently high in relationship to retained earnings and capital suggests conditions warranting a lower rating, even when earnings are at a level that might otherwise warrant a more favorable appraisal. This rating reflects not only the quantity and trend of earnings, but also factors that may affect the sustainability or quality of earnings. Regulators will consider the adequacy of transfers to the valuation reserve and the extent to which extraordinary items, securities transactions, and tax effects contribute to net income.

Earnings rated 1 are sufficient to make full provision for the absorption of losses and the accretion of capital after consideration of asset quality, growth, and other factors affecting the quality, quantity, and trend of earnings. Generally, institutions rated 1 will have earnings well above peer group averages. An institution whose earnings are relatively static or even moving downward

Financial Institutions Ratings Systems 133

may receive a 2 rating provided its level of earnings is adequate in view of asset quality, growth, and other factors affecting the quality, quantity, and trend of earnings. Normally, institutions rated 2 will have earnings that are in line with or slightly above peer group norms.

Examiners will rate an institution a 3 when its earnings are not sufficient to make full provision for the absorption of losses and the accretion of capital in relation to asset growth. The earnings pictures of 3-rated institutions may be further clouded by static or inconsistent earnings trends, chronically insufficient earnings, a high dividend payout rate, or less than satisfactory asset quality. Earnings of 3-rated institutions are generally below peer group averages.

Earnings rated 4, while generally positive, may be characterized by erratic fluctuations in net income, the development of a downward trend, intermittent losses, or a substantial drop from the previous year. Earnings of this group of institutions are ordinarily substantially below peer group averages. Institutions with earnings accorded a 5 rating are likely to be experiencing losses or reflecting a level of earnings that is worse than defined in rating number 4 above. Those losses may represent a distinct threat to the bank's solvency through the erosion of capital.

Liquidity

Regulators rate liquidity 1 through 5 with respect to:

- Adequacy of liquidity sources in light of present and future needs and the ability to meet liquidity needs of the institution without adversely affecting its operations or condition;

- Availability of assets readily convertible to cash without undue loss;

- Access to money markets and other ready sources of cash;

- Degree of reliance on short-term, volatile sources of funds, including borrowings and brokered deposits, to fund longer-term assets;

- Trend and stability of deposits; and

- Capability of management to identify, measure, monitor, and control the institution's liquidity position, including the effectiveness of funds management strategies, liquidity policies, management information systems, and contingency funding plans.

Ultimately, regulators evaluate the institution's liquidity on the basis of its capacity to meet promptly the demand for payment of its obligations and to meet the reasonable credit needs of the communities that it serves. In appraising liquidity, examiners consider the current level and prospective sources of liquidity compared to funding needs, as well as the adequacy of funds management practices relative to the institution's size, complexity, and risk profile. They will also consider, where appropriate, the overall effectiveness of asset-liability management strategies and compliance with and adequacy of established liquidity policies. The nature, volume, and anticipated usage of an institution's credit commitments are also factors examiners will weigh in arriving at an overall rating for liquidity.

A liquidity rating of 1 indicates a more than sufficient volume of liquid assets or ready and easy access on favorable terms to external sources of liquidity within the context of the institution's overall asset and liability management strategy. An institution developing a trend toward decreasing liquidity and increasing reliance on borrowed funds, yet still within acceptable proportions, may receive a 2 rating.

A 3 liquidity rating reflects an insufficient volume of liquid assets or a reliance on interest-sensitive funds that approaches or exceeds reasonable proportions for a given institution. Significant weaknesses exist in funds management practices. Ratings of 4 and 5 represent increasingly serious liquidity positions. Examiners will rate as a 5 any financial institution with liquidity positions so critical as to constitute an imminent threat to its continued viability. This group of institutions requires immediate remedial action or external financial assistance to allow them to meet their maturing obligations.

Sensitivity to Market Risk

In December 1996, the FFIEC amended the Uniform Financial Institutions Rating System to include a sixth component: sensitivity to market risk (denoted by the S in CAMELS). Generally, market risk has always been a consideration when assigning a composite rating to an institution. The principal benefit of this new component is that it provides a clearer indication of supervisory concerns related to market risk than can be gained from the former UFIRS. For example, a financial institution with weak earnings and poor liquidity also might have significant and poorly managed exposures to interest rate risk. Less than satisfactory component ratings for earnings or liquidity accorded an institution under the former ratings system would not specifically note a problem with exposure to, or the management of, market risk.

Sensitivity to market risk involves a combined assessment of a bank's level of market risk and the ability of the bank to manage that risk. Specifically, the new component reflects the degree to which changes in interest rates, foreign exchange rates, or commodity or equity prices can affect a financial institution's assets, earnings, liabilities, and capital values. The capacity of management to identify, measure, monitor, and control market risk exposure is also a factor that regulators consider.

The primary element to be considered in evaluating market risks is the sensitivity of assets, liabilities, off-balance sheet commitments, and earnings to variability in interest rates. Examiners measure this vulnerability by potential changes in earnings or economic value of capital under an appropriate range of economic scenarios.

When significant to an institution, examiners must consider the price risk related to trading and investment portfolios. If applicable, examiners also must consider the foreign exchange risk to assets, earnings, and capital because of the periodic revaluation of financial positions denominated in foreign currencies into U.S. dollar equivalents.

Regulators base the market risk rating upon these evaluation factors:

- The sensitivity of the institution's net earnings or the economic value of its capital to adverse changes in interest rates under varying economic conditions and stress environments;

- The ability of management to identify, measure, monitor, and control exposure to market risk given the institution's size, complexity, and risk profile;

- The nature and complexity of interest rate risk exposure arising from non-trading positions; and

- Where appropriate, the nature and complexity of market risk exposure arising from trading and foreign operations.

The sophistication of a bank's risk management system should correspond to the complexity of its holdings and activities and be appropriate to its specific circumstances. Institutions with relatively noncomplex holdings and activities, and with senior management actively involved in daily operations, may be able to rely on basic, less formal risk management systems. Institutions with low risk but inadequate market risk management may be subject to unfavorable ratings. Conversely, those institutions with moderate levels of market risk and a demonstrated ability to manage that risk are likely to receive favorable ratings.

A rating of 1 indicates that market risk sensitivity is well controlled and that there is minimal potential that the earnings performance or capital position will be adversely affected. Risk management practices are strong for the size, sophistication, and market risk accepted by the institution. The level of earnings and capital provide substantial support for the degree of market risk taken by the institution. Those institutions rated 2 have a moderate and controlled exposure to market risk. Risk management practices are satisfactory for the size, sophistication, and market risk accepted by the institution. The level of earnings and capital provide adequate support for the degree of market risk taken by the institution.

A rating of 3 indicates that control of market risk sensitivity needs improvement or that the potential exists for earning performance or capital position to be adversely affected. Risk management practices need to be improved given the size, sophistication, and level of market risk accepted by the institution. The level of earnings and capital may not adequately support the degree of market risk taken by the institution. A rating of 4 indicates that control of market risk sensitivity is unacceptable or that there is high potential that the earnings performance or capital position will be adversely affected. Risk management practices are deficient for the size, sophistication, and level of market risk accepted by the institution. The level of earnings and capital provide inadequate support for the degree of market risk taken by the institution. A rating of 5 indicates that control of market risk sensitivity is unacceptable or that the level of market risk taken by the institution is an imminent threat to its viability. Risk management practices are wholly inadequate for the size, sophistication, and level of market risk accepted by the institution.

CAMELS—
The FDICIA Connection

The change in the UFIRS is also an accommodation to congressional demands expressed in the FDIC Improvement Act of 1991. There are several relationships between that act and the changes the FFIEC has implemented in the rating system.

The change in the rating system adds a uniform consideration of interest rate risk. The regulators found interest rate risk impossible to measure in a convenient way applicable to all institutions through a regulation. By adding interest rate risk to the rating system, they have achieved a proxy for such a regulation that will satisfy the congressional requirement in FDICIA.

A second connection to FDICIA is the formalizing of the emphasis on capital. FDICIA installed capital as king, and the FFIEC amendment reemphasizes that fact. Capital is an explicit or implicit element of all components.

Third, the new CAMELS ratings system resembles guidelines the agencies published under the FDICIA requirement for safety and soundness guidelines. The ratings system affects all institutions, not the few the safety and soundness standards affected.

Fourth, the CAMELS ratings have a direct bearing on risk-weighted deposit insurance costs. Thus, risk management has a price. If risk management is less than satisfactory, an institution's deposit insurance costs may rise.

Finally, the changes in the ratings system invite the regulators to look forward. In keeping with the FDICIA theme of early prevention of failures, the new ratings involve the application of stress tests to an institution's market-sensitive activities.

Uniform Interagency Trust Rating System

Overview

In our discussion of the Uniform Interagency Trust Rating System ("UITRS"), we follow the regulators' consistent reference to a trust department. For purposes of this *Handbook* the reference includes limited purpose institutions holding trust powers.

The Trust Rating System is based upon an evaluation of six critical areas of a trust department's administration and operations. The composite reflects a comprehensive evaluation of the capability of the department's management, the soundness of adopted policies and procedures, the quality of service rendered to the public, and the effect of trust activities upon the soundness of the institution. The six critical areas are:

- Supervision and organization;

- Operations, controls, and audits;

- Asset administration;

- Account administration;

- Conflicts of interest; and

- Earnings, volume trends, and prospects.

Examiners rate each of these areas on the five-point scale in descending order of performance quality.

Supervision and Organization

In evaluating supervision and organization, regulators review the trust department's organization and management, including the effectiveness of director supervision and the performance and capabilities of principal officers and supporting staff.

The factors examiners will specifically consider include:

- Functional divisions of activities and personnel and the effectiveness of them;

- Technical competence, leadership, and administrative ability of senior trust management;

- Adequacy of supporting staff, including provision for any potential succession or turnover problems;

- Extent and effectiveness of director supervision, directly or through committees, care accorded the selection of committee members, and adequacy of committee minutes;

- Availability of and reliance upon competent legal counsel; and

- Sufficiency of liability insurance coverage.

A department rated 1 is well organized and managed, under effective director supervision, and supported by an experienced and competent staff that has the demonstrated ability to cope successfully with existing and foreseeable problems. A department rated 2 generally has the characteristics required for a top rating, but may have modest weaknesses in the overall level of supervision or may be fundamentally deficient in regard to management of one or more functional activities of lesser overall significance.

A department rated 3 indicates an organization and management that may be deficient in several respects. The department is generally adequate in relation to the volume and character of business administered, but management may do little in the way of effective planning and may have difficulty in responding to changing circumstances.

A department rated 4 indicates an organization that is fundamentally deficient

> The regulators are currently revising the UITRS five-point system. When the revisions are complete, UITRS will more closely resemble the language of the CAMELS rating system. Proposed changes include adding a separate risk management component as well as incorporating stronger language into the 3-rating definition.

in one or more activities of significant overall importance. Management may be inexperienced or inattentive and may lack the ability to respond reasonably to changing circumstances or to correct less than satisfactory conditions.

A department rated 5 indicates organizational weaknesses and managerial incompetence of such severity as to warrant immediate action if sound conditions are to be achieved.

Operations, Controls, and Audits

In evaluating this area examiners consider the department's operational systems and controls in relation to its volume and character of business. They will also review the adequacy of audit coverage designed to assure the integrity of the financial records and the sufficiency of internal controls.

The factors regulators will specifically consider include:

- The adequacy of facilities, systems, and records;

- The effectiveness of controls and safeguards including segregation of duties, vault controls, and security movement controls;

- The scope, frequency, and quality of audits (internal or external) and reports;

- Where applicable, the qualifications and capability of internal auditors; and

- The independence and access of auditors to the board of directors.

In a department rated 1, operations are efficient, effectively controlled, and subject to comprehensive internal or external audits, as the circumstances of the department may require.

A 2-rated department has characteristics similar to those necessary for a top rating, but modest weaknesses exist that are readily correctable in the normal course of business.

A 3-rated department is one that may be fundamentally deficient in respect to one or more activities of lesser importance. On an overall basis its operating practices and audits are adequate in relation to the volume and character of business it conducts.

A 4-rated department makes little provision for audits of any kind or has weak or potentially dangerous operating practices in combination with infrequent or inadequate audits.

In a 5-rated department examiners will find operating practices, with or without audits, that pose a serious threat to the safeguarding of funds and securities.

Asset Administration

In evaluating this area, regulators will consider policies, practices, and procedures relating to the selection, retention, and preservation of assets. They will review methods the department uses to review, protect, and make productive the various types of assets composing the trust department's aggregate portfolio.

Examiners will specifically consider these factors:

- The adequacy of the investment selection and retention process, including provision for committee approval and extent of compliance with it;

- The availability of an approved list of investments and a system of approval for deviations from it;

- The sources and quality of advice and research and adequacy of documentation to support decisions on investment and retention;

- As applicable, the quality of administration accorded collective investment funds, master notes, real estate, mortgage loans, closely held corporations, and other asset holdings requiring special expertise; and

- The general quality of asset holdings and sufficiency of supporting documentation.

A 1 rating denotes superior performance in all respects; policies and procedures are well-conceived and appropriate to the effective administration of asset holdings. The responsibility for asset holdings is of demonstrable fiduciary quality and it is supported by sufficient research documentation to demonstrate prudent judgment.

A 2-rated department shows generally superior or above-average performance that is flawed only by modest weaknesses in policies and procedures, in asset quality, or in the adequacy of supporting documentation.

In a 3-rated department, asset administration may be flawed by a moderate degree of weakness in supporting documentation or by inadequate or even nonexistent policies and procedures. Generally, the department follows conservative investment practices which pose little or no threat to the trust beneficiaries.

A 4 rating characterizes asset administration that is notably deficient in relation

Financial Institutions Ratings Systems 141

to the volume and character of responsibility for asset holdings. The deficiency may show up in the selection or retention of numerous securities or other assets of doubtful fiduciary quality.

A 5 rating characterizes administrative practices that flagrantly disregard the department's fiduciary obligation to preserve and make productive the trust assets. Examiners may conclude that continuation of those practices could jeopardize the interests of the account beneficiaries generally and could result in surcharge to the institution.

Account Administration

In reviewing account administration, regulators consider the trust department's policies, practices, and procedures relating to the administration of its accounts.

Factors examiners specifically consider include:

- The soundness of adopted policies and procedures and the extent of compliance with them;

- The use of synopsis sheets, familiarity of personnel with account circumstances, and timeliness of administrative actions;

- The administrative consideration accorded acceptance and termination of accounts, cash balances, and overdrafts, and discretionary distributions of income and principal, including provision for committee approval;

- The process of selection and periodic review of account assets for suitability (in terms of diversification and other investment characteristics), and for conformity with instrument provisions and account objectives, including provision for committee approval;

- The familiarity and compliance with applicable laws and regulations; and

- As applicable, the policies and procedures relating to the acceptance and review of direction trusts and other accounts of a unique or unusual nature.

A department rated 1 shows superior performance in all respects. Its policies and procedures are well conceived and appropriately implemented. It administers individual accounts in conformance with the specific investment and retention powers of the governing instrument or the statutory or case law of the jurisdiction, and in accordance with sound fiduciary principles. A department with a 2 rating shows generally superior or above-average performance that is flawed only by modest weaknesses in policies, procedures, or practices. Any corrective action will occur without loss to the fiduciary accounts.

A department with a 3 rating may show performance that is flawed by a lack of adequate policies and procedures. Its administrative practices are generally acceptable in relation to the volume and character of accounts under administration.

A 4-rated department has account administration that is notably deficient, as evidenced by a failure to adhere to sound administrative practices or the frequent occurrence of violations of laws, regulations, or terms of the governing instruments.

A 5-rated department shows neglectful or incompetent administration through its flagrant or repeated disregard of laws, regulations, or terms of the governing instruments, or significant departures from sound administrative practices.

Conflicts of Interest

In evaluating this area examiners consider the significance of potential conflicts and self-dealing and the adequacy of policies and procedures designed to minimize the potential for resulting abuses. They will evaluate the adequacy of policies and procedures in light of the size of the trust department and the character of its business. They will also consider the extent of potential and actual conflicts in relation to other departments of similar character and size, and the sensitivity management demonstrates in attempting to refrain from self-dealing, in minimizing potential conflicts, and in resolving actual conflicts in favor of the fiduciary accounts.

The factors examiners will specifically consider include:

- The adequacy of policies and procedures designed to minimize principal and income cash on deposit in the department's own bank;

- The department's holding of the stock of its own bank, holding company, or its affiliates and the adequacy of policies and procedures relating to the acquisition, retention, and voting of that stock;

- The volume of related commercial and trust relationships and of holdings of corporations in which directors, officers, or employees of the bank may be interested and the adequacy of policies and procedures designed to encourage investment decision-making without improper regard to the interests of commercial banking customers or bank directors, officers, and employees;

- The adequacy of policies and procedures designed to prevent the improper use of material inside information;

- The adequacy of securities trading policies and practices relating to such matters as the allocation of brokerage business, the payment for services with "soft dollars" and the combining, crossing, and timing of trades; and

- The instances and aspects of policies and procedures relating to any matters of self-dealing and inter-trust dealing.

A department rated 1 will have adopted and effectively implemented a comprehensive conflict of interest policy statement dealing in adequate fashion with the full range of potential conflicts and self-dealing. A department rated 1 will be reasonably successful in minimizing the incidents of potential conflicts and will always resolve actual conflicts in favor of the fiduciary accounts.

In a department rated 2, examiners will find moderate weaknesses in policies and procedures, but the record will affirm management's determination to minimize the instances of abuse.

A 3-rated department will show a few positive efforts to minimize potential conflicts. It will refrain from self-dealing, but it will not be regularly confronted with either potential or actual conflicts of any significance.

In a department rated 4, there will be little or no attempt to minimize potential conflicts or to refrain from self-dealing. A 4-rated department will be confronted with a notable degree of potential or actual conflicts.

A 5-rated department is one that demonstrates a flagrant disregard for the interests of the trust beneficiaries or frequently engages in transactions that compromise its fundamental duty of undivided loyalty to the trust beneficiaries.

Earnings, Volume Trends, and Prospects

In reviewing this area, examiners will evaluate the department's operating results and earnings trends. They will also consider the probable effect on earnings of the volume and character of present and anticipated future business.

The factors examiners will specifically consider include:

- Management's attitude toward growth and new business development;

- The department's dependency upon nonrecurring fees and commissions;

- Any unusual features regarding the composition of business, fee schedules, and the effects of charge-offs or compromise actions; and

- New business development efforts, including such factors as types of business solicited, market potential, advertising, competition, and relationships with local organizations.

In a 1-rated department, operations in each of the past five years will have been profitable without credit for deposit balances. In addition, business volume and prospects will favor a continuation of this trend.

In a 2-rated department, operating results for the past five years reflect, on average, a net profit without credit for deposit balances. Although an occasional loss year is possible, business volume and prospects will favor a continuation of five-year average profitability.

In a 3-rated department, operations are generally unprofitable. Operating losses, when averaged over the previous five-year period, do not exceed the average credit for deposit balances. Gross revenues will be generally sufficient to permit recovery of salary expenses and projections indicate they will continue to do so.

In a 4-rated department, operating losses, when averaged over the previous five-year period, do not exceed the average credit for deposit balances, but gross revenues are generally not sufficient to permit recovery of salary expenses. Business volume and prospects suggest a continuation of this trend.

In a 5-rated department, operating losses consistently exceed the credit for deposit balances. No reversal of this trend appears likely.

In applying the rating guidelines, regulators will emphasize not only existing levels of profitability or unprofitability, but also the department's new business development efforts and competitive and other market factors in order to determine whether current earnings trends are likely to continue. For example, a department that has been clearly profitable in each of the past five years on the basis of operations may have allowed its performance or its new business efforts to deteriorate to the point where there may be serious doubt whether the department can sustain profitability. In this case, an examiner may assign a rating one step lower than that called for by application of the guidelines. Conversely, a department that has narrowed its losses over the past five years may warrant a rating one step above that called for by application of the guidelines where volume trends and prospects suggest continuing improvement in the earnings trend.

In smaller departments where expenses are not allocated, an examiner will estimate both total expenses and the credit for deposit balances.

Some small part-time departments operate at a loss and are in business primarily for the purpose of providing full banking services to customers. For those departments, examiners have discretion to rate Earnings, Volume Trends, and Prospects as a "4" without regard to the credit for deposit balances.

Proposed Rule

In February 1998, the FFIEC proposed changes to UITRS. The proposed changes include:

- Realigning the UITRS rating definitions to make them conform to the UFIRS definitions;

- Reducing the component rating categories from six to five;

- Making the earnings rating optional at the federal supervisory agency's discretion;

- Referring to the quality of risk management processes in the management component; and

- Identifying the risk elements within the composite and component rating definitions.

A brief summary of the proposal follows.

Under the current UITRS, regulators consider a composite rated 3 trust department to be generally adequate. A composite rated 3 bank under UFIRS demonstrates some degree of supervisory concern. The proposal brings the UITRS composite 3 rating into line with the UFIRS rating.

The proposal will eliminate the current Account Administration and Conflicts of Interest components and replace these components with a Compliance component. The new component will address all areas previously addressed in the Account Administration and Conflicts of Interest components. In addition, the Compliance component will address compliance with applicable laws, regulations, and internal policies and procedures on an institutionwide basis.

The FFIEC recognizes that many small institutions offer fiduciary services as a service to the community with profitability as a secondary consideration. The proposal requires the examiners to continue to evaluate fiduciary earnings at all institutions. A federal supervisory agency may decide not to require an earnings ratings for institutions with less than $100 million in total assets, as long as the institution is not a nondeposit trust company.

The proposal includes changes to each component reflecting the FFIEC's emphasis on risk management processes. Language in each component emphasizes that examiners must consider processes to identify, measure, monitor, and control risks. The FFIEC proposes to identify the types of risks associated with each of the component ratings explicitly. The proposal also includes specific references to the quality of overall risk management in the composite rating definitions to reflect changes in the component rating definitions.

The FFIEC must follow administrative procedure by accepting and considering comments on the proposal. Managers of financial institutions should expect the revised UITRS to be very similar to the proposed UITRS. The FFIEC is virtually certain to align UITRS more closely to the CAMELS standards and increase the emphasis on management of risks.

Ratings of Foreign Banking Organizations

Overview

In passing the Foreign Bank Supervision Enhancement Act in 1991, Congress required an annual examination of U.S. branches and agencies of foreign banks and increased the authority of the Federal Reserve Board to conduct these examinations. The Federal Reserve replaced the states and the OCC as the principal regulator of foreign banks in the U.S.

While the Federal Reserve is the principal regulator, it works in conjunction with the other regulatory agencies and conducts joint examinations of state licensed offices with the state supervisor. Thus, late in 1994, the Board, OCC, FDIC, New York Superintendent of Banks, and other state regulators announced the adoption of a new examination and supervisory program for foreign bank operations in the United States that established a three-tiered rating system for foreign banking organizations' operations in the United States.

The ROCA Rating

The first step in the three-tiered rating system is the appropriate regulator's assignment of a **ROCA** rating to each branch or agency of a foreign bank. The rating is an assessment of the branch or agency's:

- Risk management;

- Operational controls;

Financial Institutions Ratings Systems 147

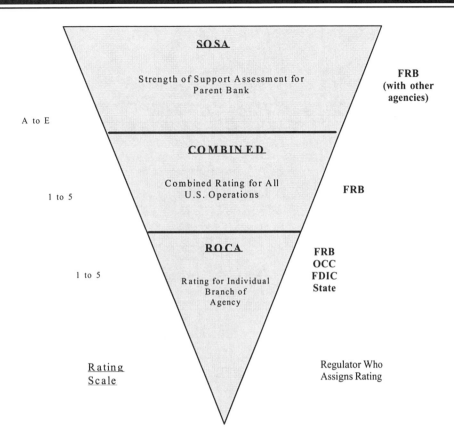

- Compliance; and
- Asset quality.

The three-tiered rating system is presented in the table above.

The federal or state regulator conducting the examination of a particular branch or agency assigns the ROCA rating. The regulators assign ratings on the five-point scale. The meanings of the 1 to 5 ratings are parallel to the definitions discussed above in the Introduction to this section of the *Handbook*. Thus, ratings of 1 and 2 merit only normal supervision. Rating 3 requires more supervisory attention, but does not pose a threat to its customers, the payments system, or the insurance fund. Ratings 4 and 5 require intense supervisory attention.

The following tables present a graphic explanation of the ratings.

Since January 1, 1997, examiners disclose ROCA component ratings to senior management and directors in an effort to better focus management's attention on possible areas of weakness and the need for timely corrective actions.

ROCA Composite Ratings

1	**Strong** branch or agency in every respect. Normal supervisory attention required.
2	**Modest weaknesses** correctable by management. Normal supervisory attention required.
3	**Significant weaknesses** in management, controls, and compliance or numerous asset quality problems in combination with condition of parent or other factors. Closer supervisory attention required.
4	**Marginal condition** due to serious problems or weaknesses. Close supervisory attention and definite plan for corrective action required.
5	**Unsatisfactory condition** due to severe weaknesses. Urgent restructuring of operations required.

ROCA Composite Ratings

Rating	Risk management	Operational Controls	Compliance	Asset Quality
1	Fully integrated	Comprehensive	Outstanding	Strong
2	Modest weaknesses	Satisfactory	Sufficient	Satisfactory
3	Lacking	Lacking	Significant deficiencies	Fair
4	Serious weaknesses	Serious deficiencies	Insufficient attention	Marginal
5	Critical deficiencies	Serious jeopardy	Unsatisfactory	Unsatisfactory

The Combined Rating

As a second step, the Federal Reserve will assign a **Combined** rating for those foreign banks with U.S. banking offices supervised by more than one bank regulatory agency or that have significant nonbanking activities in the United States. In assigning the rating, the Board takes into consideration:

- All elements of the ROCA rating system;

- The quality of risk management employed by all levels of the foreign bank in the United States; and

- The result of actual examinations or inspections of bank and nonbank offices or subsidiaries.

The Combined rating is also on a scale of 1 to 5, with ratings of 1 and 2 meriting only normal supervision. Unlike the ROCA rating, examiners communicate this Combined rating only to the foreign bank's head office and to other U.S. supervisors. The rating is otherwise confidential.

The SOSA Rating

Third, a foreign bank is assigned a **SOSA** rating, which is a Strength Of Support Assessment of the parent foreign bank's ability to manage effectively and stand behind and support its U.S. operations. The Federal Reserve Board, in consultation with the other federal and state bank regulatory agencies, assigns the SOSA rating. The SOSA rating has two components.

The first component addresses whether any factors relating to the ability of the foreign bank to meet its U.S. obligations warrant special monitoring of U.S. operations. It is, in general terms, based on the foreign bank's financial condition and external home country factors, including the adequacy of home country supervision, the willingness of the home country to stand behind its banking system, and transfer risk. This component is rated on a scale of A to E, with A and B representing only normal levels of supervisory concern.

	SOSA Ratings
A.	Strong institution and comprehensive oversight by home country supervisor.
B.	Institution is investment grade; significant degree of supervisory oversight.
C.	Institution may not meet all international standards for capital, etc.; home country has demonstrated willingness and ability to support.
D.	Significant financial or supervisory weaknesses; imposition of asset maintenance requirements should be considered at U.S. branches and agencies.
E.	Seriously deficient financial profile; absence of significant supervisory oversight and support; institution may be unable to honor its obligations.

The Board uses the second SOSA component on an as-needed basis to identify whether there are any factors that raise questions about the foreign bank's ability to maintain adequate internal controls and compliance procedures over its U.S. operations. Should the Board find the existence of these control risks at a foreign bank, it will place an asterisk next to the letter rating.

U.S. regulators use SOSA ratings for internal supervisory purposes. The rating is not disclosed to the foreign bank or its home country supervisor. The SOSA rating is based, for the most part, on information provided in a foreign bank's annual report to the Board, on a publicly available rating and other information, on significant accounting policies in the home country, and on "visits" by regulatory staff with the parent foreign bank and its home country regulators. These home country visits are information-gathering exercises by U.S. regulatory authorities and are not meant to be viewed in any way as an inspection or examination of a foreign bank's home office.

In February 1995, the Board published an *Examination Manual for U.S. Branches and Agencies of Foreign Banks* that the Board and Federal Reserve Bank supervisory staff jointly prepared. In preparing the manual they received substantial contributions from the New York State Banking Department, the OCC, FDIC, and other state supervisors. The manual explains not only the new rating and examination system for foreign banks but, it also sets forth examination objectives, procedures, internal control questionnaires, and audit guidelines for implementing the new system.

Annual Examination Plan

> U.S. regulators have recently announced that risk management will be an increasingly important focus of U.S. examinations of both domestic and foreign banks (see the Risk Focused Examinations section of this *Handbook*).

In furtherance of the new Combined rating for all U.S. operations of a foreign bank, the Board develops an Annual Examination Plan for each foreign bank. The Board obtains input from the other federal and state regulators involved and is responsible for coordinating its implementation. Under this plan, each branch or agency should be subject to only one safety and soundness examination per year by a federal or state regulator, either singly or in a joint examination. As overall regulator of all of a foreign bank's U.S. operations, the Board may participate in an examiner meeting with management at the close of an examination, where examiners have found that possible systemic weaknesses may exist. To the greatest extent possible, the Board is seeking to coordinate examinations so that all of a foreign bank's offices in different states will be examined simultaneously.

In the case of branches and agencies of foreign banks, examiners rating the Risk Management factor of ROCA are looking for:

- A fully integrated risk management system that has defined limits and guidelines for risk exposure, and comprehensive risk assessment; and

- A strong Management Information System integrated with head office to monitor risks.

In rating the Operational Controls Element of ROCA, examiners are focusing on effective internal controls and audit procedures, appropriate head office supervision, and timely reporting systems.

With respect to U.S. bank (or thrift) subsidiaries of foreign banking organizations, examiners will also be focusing on comprehensive risk management policies and procedures and strong internal control structures. Risk management will be an important element in rating the management component of a U.S. bank under the CAMELS system.

Satisfactory risk management ratings are important to strategic expansion objectives in the U.S. market, as an increasing number of laws, as well as agency practice, require an institution to be "well-managed" to receive regulatory approvals for any significant expansion of its operations or lines of business.

The Bank Holding Company Rating System — BOPEC

Overview

The bank holding company rating system is a management information and supervisory tool that defines the condition of bank holding companies in a systematic way. In employing the system, the Federal Reserve evaluates each bank holding company through a review of its components. The Federal Reserve:

- Evaluates the financial condition and risk characteristics of each major component of the bank holding company;

- Assesses the important interrelationships among the components; and

- Analyzes the strength and significance of key consolidated financial and operating performance characteristics.

This methodology emphasizes the Federal Reserve's doctrine that holding companies are to be a source of financial and managerial strength to their bank subsidiaries. To arrive at an overall assessment of financial condition, the Federal Reserve evaluates these elements of the bank holding company:

- Bank subsidiaries;

- Other (nonbank) subsidiaries;

- Parent company;

- Earnings — Consolidated; and

- Capital Adequacy — Consolidated.

Risk Management

The BOPEC rating is the acronym derived from the first letters of each of the original five elements. As with most of the other systems of ratings, BOPEC is on the five-point scale with one the highest rating and five the lowest. Since January 1, 1997, examiners disclose both component and composite BOPEC ratings in summary sections of examination reports to senior officials and boards of directors of bank holding companies.

The first three elements of the BOPEC rating, i.e., the bank, other subsidiaries, and parent company, reflect the contribution of each to the fundamental financial soundness of the holding company. The rating of consolidated earnings, capital, and risk management recognizes the importance that regulators place on these factors and their crucial role in maintaining the financial strength and supporting the risk characteristics of the entire organization.

The ability and competence of holding company management have an important bearing on every aspect of holding company operations. Consequently, the Federal Reserve includes that factor in the evaluation of each of the principal elements of the bank holding company rating, as well as in the assignment of an overall holding company rating.

In addition to the individual elements described above, the Federal Reserve assigns each company an overall or composite rating, which has both a financial and managerial component. The financial composite rating is an overall evaluation of the ratings of each of the five principal elements of the holding company's operations as defined above. The financial composite rating is also based upon a scale of one through five in descending order of performance quality.

The managerial composite is a comprehensive evaluation of holding company management as reflected in the conduct of the affairs of the bank and nonbank subsidiaries and the parent company. The managerial composite is indicated by the assignment of a letter rating, "S", "F", or "U." Respectively those letters mean that the Federal Reserve has found management to be satisfactory, fair, or unsatisfactory.

The complete rating represents a summary evaluation of the bank holding company in the form of a rating fraction. The numerator of that fraction reflects the condition of the principal components of the holding company and assessments of certain key consolidated financial and operating factors. The denominator represents the composite rating, as defined in greater detail below, including both its financial and managerial components.

While the elements in the numerator represent the essential foundation upon which the composite rating is based, the composite does not reflect a simple arithmetic mean or rigid formula weighting of the individual performance dimensions. In the view of the Federal Reserve, any kind of formula could be misleading and inappropriate. Rather, the composite reflects the examiner's judgment of the overall condition of the bank holding company based upon his knowledge and experience with the company. Thus, the complete rating is displayed as follows:

BOPEC
FM

The bank holding company rating system parallels the uniform interagency bank rating system to some degree by employing similar rating scales and performance definitions to evaluate both the individual elements and the summary or overall condition of the holding company. By using this framework, the Federal Reserve intends to provide for consistency and facilitate the adoption and use of the holding company rating system. The rating system is also sufficiently flexible to allow for appropriate differences in appraising shell bank holding companies.

Shell bank holding companies make up the majority of supervised bank holding companies, and involve a substantial volume of banking assets, thus, the rating system must also address them. For shell bank holding companies, the Federal Reserve follows a procedure similar to that so far described. However, in evaluating a shell bank holding company, the examiner assigns a 0 rating for many of the BOPEC elements: the other (nonbank) subsidiaries, consolidated earnings, and consolidated capital. The result is that the rating is made up of these elements for a shell bank holding company:

- The numerator reflects only the ratings of the bank and the parent (with emphasis on cash flow and debt servicing ability), bank; and

- The denominator includes both the financial and managerial elements of the composite rating.

For purposes of the rating, the FRB defines shell companies as bank holding companies that have total consolidated assets less than $150 million *and* that have no significant nonbank subsidiaries. For companies of $150 million or more in assets with no significant nonbank subsidiaries the examiners will assign a "0" for the "other subsidiary" component of the rating.

For nonshell companies under $150 million in consolidated assets with significant nonbank assets, the examiners will assign a rating that includes a component for the nonbank subsidiaries. Thus, these nonshell companies' ratings will include the bank, other nonbank, and parent components, but may exclude consolidated earnings and capital ratings if the needed figures for them are not available. As this scheme suggests, the FRB rates elements whenever they are relevant for a particular company. In practice, this means that:

- All companies with $150 million or more in consolidated assets should be given a complete rating;

- Shell companies should receive a rating for the bank and parent components and both composites; and

- Nonshell companies under $150 million in assets *with* significant nonbank operating subsidiaries should receive a rating that includes a nonbank component.

The FRB gives the examiner discretion to include ratings of consolidated earnings and capital for nonshell companies, if the figures are available or if they are necessary to reflect overall condition.

Financial Composite Rating

The Federal Reserve defines the five composite ratings in words that closely parallel those of the CAMELS and UITRS systems. Therefore the ratings can be described in this shorthand:

- Composite 1 — Sound in almost every respect;

- Composite 2 — Fundamentally sound, limited supervision required;

- Composite 3 — A combination of weaknesses which pose only a limited threat to the company's viability, more than normal supervision required;

- Composite 4 — An immoderate volume of asset weaknesses, or a combination of other conditions that are less than satisfactory requiring close supervision; and

- Composite 5 — The weaknesses are so critical as to require urgent aid from shareholders or other sources to prevent insolvency; these companies require immediate corrective action and constant supervisory attention.

Management Composite Rating

The management rating reflects an examiner's overall evaluation of the capabilities and competence of the management of the parent company and senior management of the bank(s) and nonbank subsidiaries. The assessment of management will be unique to each holding company, reflecting its particular situation. Business complexities and operating problems vary with the size and type of holding company activity; management that is competent to effectively discharge responsibilities under one set of conditions may be less competent as these conditions change. In addition to objective operating results, regulators use important subjective considerations in assessing management performance include the following:

1. Ability to identify and control major sources of risk;

2. Technical competence, leadership, administrative ability and oversight, management depth, and succession;

3. Knowledge of and compliance with the Bank Holding Company Act and related regulations, and all other relevant laws and regulations;

4. History of serving the banking needs of the community;

5. Ability to plan and respond to changing circumstances;

6. Ability of parent management to monitor and direct subsidiary operations in order to ensure prudent operation and compliance with established holding company policies;

7. Adequacy and scope of internal audit systems and controls and evaluation of them as contained in audit reports; and

8. Attitude toward risk as indicated by any undue reliance on resources of subsidiary bank(s) to support nonbank activities.

A rating of satisfactory (S) indicates a management that is fully effective with respect to almost all factors. Management is responsive and has the ability to cope successfully with existing and foreseeable problems that may arise in the conduct of the parent's or subsidiaries' affairs. Management rated satisfactory is knowledgeable concerning relevant laws and regulations, and has demonstrated an understanding of the need to insulate the subsidiary bank(s) from any undue risk associated with nonbank activities.

A rating of fair (F) reflects performance that is lacking in some measure of ability that would be desirable to meet responsibilities necessitated by various situations that management must address. Either management has modest talent when above-average abilities are called for, or it is distinctly below average for the type and size of organization in which it operates. Thus, its responsiveness or ability to correct less than satisfactory conditions may be lacking. Management rated fair may reflect a less than satisfactory understanding of relevant holding company laws and regulations.

A rating of unsatisfactory (U) indicates a management that is demonstrably inferior or incompetent in relation to the responsibilities or problems it faces. The U rating may also indicate that management is inclined to subject the subsidiary bank(s) to excessive or unwarranted risk as a result of the activities of the nonbank subsidiaries. Problems resulting from management weakness are so severe that management must be strengthened or replaced before the company can return to a sound condition.

Performance Evaluation

The Federal Reserve evaluates the components of holding company operations (bank subsidiaries, nonbank subsidiaries, parent only, consolidated earnings, capital, and risk management) on the five-point scale.

9. Rating No. 1 — Strong performance that is significantly higher than average. There is no need for supervisory concern.

10. Rating No. 2 — Satisfactory performance that is average or above that adequately provides for the safe and sound operation of the bank holding company and its subsidiaries.

11. Rating No. 3 — Fair performance that is neither satisfactory nor marginal but is characterized by performance of below average quality requiring management attention to prevent further deterioration.

12. Rating No. 4 — Marginal performance that is significantly below average which, if unchecked, might evolve into conditions that could threaten the viability of the institution.

13. Rating No. 5 — Unsatisfactory performance that is critically deficient and in need of immediate remedial attention. This level of performance by itself, or in combination with other weaknesses, could threaten the viability of the institution.

Bank Condition

The bank condition component reflects the overall condition of the banking subsidiary or subsidiaries. For this purpose, examiners use the subsidiary bank CAMELS composite rating(s). For multibank companies, they will weight each bank's composite rating according to its asset size to arrive at an average bank composite rating. Weighting implies that, in most cases, the bank condition component in the holding company rating system will usually reflect the lead bank's composite according to the bank rating system (CAMELS).

A problem bank could go unnoticed in a multibank holding company whose bank condition component, based on weighted averages, is acceptable (i.e., bank condition ratings of 1, 2, or 3). To highlight the presence of a 4- or 5-rated bank in the multibank system, the Federal Reserve attaches a problem identifier, "P", to the bank condition rating (e.g., 1P, 2P, 3P). For example, a 2P condition rating indicates that the banking subsidiaries are generally rated satisfactory but a problem bank (composite 4 or 5) exists among the banking subsidiaries. Although the bank condition component is a weighted average, it can be adjusted for subjective, judgmental reasons at the discretion of the examiner.

Other (Nonbank) Subsidiaries

The other subsidiaries rating is an assessment of the condition of the nonbank subsidiaries in the context of their overall impact on the financial condition of the holding company and the subsidiary bank(s).

The examiner emphasizes the asset quality of credit — extending subsidiaries and the profitability and operating soundness of noncredit-extending subsidiaries in making this rating. The other subsidiaries evaluation requires the regulator to concentrate on the quality and condition of these nonbank assets:

- The underlying assets of credit-extending nonbank subsidiaries; and

- The parent's investment in and advances to noncredit-extending subsidiaries.

Poorly run servicing or other noncredit-extending subsidiaries can pose significant risk exposure to the holding company, thus the Federal Reserve requires a review of the flow of funds to these subsidiaries. These subsidiaries can expose the parent to the risks of operating losses or off-balance sheet items, such as guarantees. In many cases, because noncredit-extending subsidiaries are not heavy borrowers from external sources, the examiner will use the parent's investments in and advances to these companies as a proxy for the size of their operations.

The Federal Reserve will quantify the degree of risk associated with the noncredit-extending subsidiaries by classifying the parent's investments in and advances to those subsidiaries if the examiner can meaningfully classify the financial condition of the subsidiaries or the characteristics of their assets. This classification might occur, for instance, if the subsidiaries' historical earnings records have not, in the examiner's judgment, adequately accounted for the development of clearly identifiable loss potential associated with the entity's operations. If the examiner cannot make a conventional classification of the investments in or advances to the noncredit-extending subsidiaries, the examiner will analyze the risk exposure posed by the noncredit-extending subsidiaries. The analysis will parallel that for any asset appraisal, with the examiner giving particular attention to the subsidiary's purpose and operating efficiency, management reporting procedures, and profitability. Foreign subsidiaries are subject to the same assessment.

For evaluating the risk associated with credit-extending subsidiaries, the regulator will look to the classification of the underlying assets of the subsidiaries. The weights assigned to problem investments and classified assets reflect the severity of their problems: 100 percent of "loss," 50 percent of "doubtful," and 20 percent of "substandard."

In rating nonbank activities, the examiner's first step is to appraise their significance to the company's overall financial performance. The appraisal should focus on the potential loss exposure these activities pose to the bank holding company. As a general rule, the Federal Reserve will rate other subsidiaries whenever nonbank assets exceed 5 percent of consolidated capital or $10 million, whichever is lower. The examiner may rate other subsidiary assets that do not meet the significance conditions if not to do so would significantly misrepresent the condition of the holding company.

In rating nonbank activities, the examiner considers:

14. The relationship of problem investments in and advances to noncredit-extending subsidiaries plus classified assets in the credit-extending nonbank subsidiaries to total nonbank assets;

15. The relationship of problem investments and advances plus classified assets to the sum of parent company and nonbank valuation reserves and ex-bank consolidated equity capital, or other appropriate measure;

16. The ability of nonbank management to supervise and exercise overall control over nonbank subsidiary operations complying with sound asset administration, and established holding company policies and relevant laws and regulations; and

17. Management attitudes toward risk as indicated by any undue reliance on resources of affiliated bank(s) to support nonbank subsidiaries.

In addition the examiner may consider other relevant factors such as profitability, operating efficiency, management controls, reporting procedures, and any other relevant factors that may be necessary to assess the condition of the nonbank subsidiaries.

An asset quality rating of 1 indicates sound, well-managed nonbank operations, investments, and loan portfolios raising no supervisory concerns.

A 2 rating indicates the existence of some asset problems or other minor operational weaknesses warranting minimal supervisory concern. Problems associated with a 2 rating can readily be resolved in the normal course of business.

A 3 rating represents the existence of deficiencies that, if left unchecked, could cause substantial deterioration and have an adverse impact on the banking subsidiaries.

A 4 rating represents an increased need for supervisory surveillance and concern due to any combination of poor operations, weak management, or severe asset problems affecting the holding company or the banking subsidiaries.

A 5 rating applies to a critical level of nonbank problems.

Parent Company

The parent company rating reflects a parent company's ability to service its debt and other fixed obligations. It is also an evaluation of the quality of direct parent credit extensions to entities that are not subsidiaries of the holding company.

In analyzing the parent company, the Federal Reserve will consider its ability to generate adequate cash flow from its ongoing operations and the liquidity of its assets. The analysis also takes into account the capacity of the parent company to safely obtain liquidity from its subsidiaries by, for example, the prudent upstreaming of additional subsidiary dividends.

The examiner will analyze these factors:

18. The volume and composition of parent company debt, and resulting cash flow needs;

19. The maturities of parent company borrowings compared with the maturities of the investments that they fund;

20. The quality of credits to nonaffiliated companies;

21. The parent's ability to convert assets readily to cash without incurring serious loss or adversely affecting the banking subsidiaries;

22. Management's ability to plan for liquidity and cash flow needs and respond to changing conditions in the markets for short-term funds;

23. The company's ability to obtain long- and short-term funds on reasonable terms, and the existence of firm backup lines of credit;

24. The reasonableness of any management or service fees a bank subsidiary pays to the parent;

25. The company's performance in meeting past and current servicing requirements; and

26. Parent management's ability to ensure prudent operation, sound asset administration, and compliance with established holding company policies and relevant laws and regulations.

Examiners will review a shell company in a similar manner. The major consideration in a shell company is cash flow to service parent company debt because of the likely effect on the subsidiary bank's capital position. In addition, the examiner will compare the amount of parent company debt to the parent's proportionate interest in the subsidiary bank's equity capital.

A parent company rating of 1 indicates that the holding company can readily generate cash flow that is more than adequate to service its debt obligations and other cash flow needs and provide for the smooth rollover of debt without adverse affect on its subsidiaries.

The rating also reflects good management and the absence of significant asset problems.

A 2 rating, while reflecting a fundamentally sound situation, indicates a possible trend toward tighter liquidity due to lower earnings, asset quality, or other relevant operating indices.

A rating of 3 represents a decidedly tight, but still manageable, cash flow situation. The company will likely have little or no liquidity in its asset portfolio or it may be overly dependent on potentially harmful dividends and fees from its subsidiaries. The 3 rating reflects increasing difficulty for the parent company in obtaining short-term funds on favorable terms.

A rating of 4 indicates serious cash flow problems because of severe asset deterioration or poor or no corporate earnings. Companies rated 4 may be seriously draining funds from bank subsidiaries to service cash flow needs and may be completely unable to serve as a source of funds or financial strength to their subsidiaries.

A rating of 5 may represent an inability to enter money markets. The problems represented by a rating of 5 reflect an imminent danger of default or insolvency of the parent company.

Earnings — Consolidated

The Federal Reserve bases the rating of earnings on the assessment of fully consolidated profitability. Fully consolidated profitability serves as a source of financial strength and capital growth for the entire organization.

Profitability has two dimensions, quantity and quality, both of which an examiner will incorporate into the evaluation of earnings. Quantity refers to the absolute level of net income and its adequacy in relation to the considerations listed below. The appraisal of quality is an attempt to determine the strength of operating earnings and the degree to which earnings reflect the impact of unusually large securities gains or losses, unusual tax items, or other large, nonrecurring, extraordinary gains or losses. Quality of earnings also refers to the effect on net income of adequately providing additions to the loan loss reserve in order to properly recognize the impact of poor, overstated, or loss assets carried on the balance sheet. In the judgment of the Federal Reserve, consolidated net income that relies unduly on unusually large, nonrecurring gains or that fails to reflect adequate loan loss provisions is of lower quality than net income of equal magnitude that reflects strong operations and adequate loss provisions.

Generally, an examiner will rate consolidated earnings since the prior inspection with emphasis given to the most recent year's performance. The considerations in the earnings evaluation are:

27. The return on consolidated assets, historical earnings trends, and peer group comparisons;

28. The quality of earnings as reflected by the extent of reliance on nonrecurring gains or losses or unusual tax effects and the sufficiency of loss provisions in view of the condition of the asset portfolio and the adequacy of the loan loss reserves;

29. The ability to cover chargeoffs, maintain public confidence, and provide for the safe ongoing operation of the company;

30. Management's ability to plan and devise realistic earnings projections in light of the risk structure and quality of assets;

31. The outlook for earnings as implied by the current risk structure and quality of assets; and

32. The ability of earnings to provide for the growth of capital in light of recent and planned asset growth.

Earnings rated 1 are sufficient to make full provision for the absorption of losses and accretion of capital after considering asset quality and bank holding company growth. Generally, 1-rated holding companies will have earnings well above peer group averages.

A company whose earnings are relatively static or even moving downward may receive a 2 rating provided its level of earnings is adequate to absorb losses and build capital. A company with a 2 rating will have earnings that are in line with or slightly above peer group norms.

A 3 should be accorded earnings that are not fully adequate to make sufficient provisions for the absorption of losses and the accretion of capital in relation to company growth. The earnings pictures of such companies may be further clouded by static or inconsistent earnings trends, chronically insufficient earnings, or less than satisfactory asset quality.

Earnings rated 4, while generally positive, are clearly not adequate to make full provision for losses and the necessary accretion of capital. Companies with earnings rated 4 may be characterized by erratic fluctuations in net income, poor earnings (and the likelihood of the development of a further downward trend), intermittent losses, chronically depressed earnings, or a substantial drop from the previous year. Earnings of 4-rated companies are ordinarily substantially below peer group averages.

Bank holding companies with earnings accorded a 5 rating are experiencing losses or reflecting a level of earnings that, if not reversed, could represent a distinct threat to the holding company's solvency through the erosion of capital.

Capital Adequacy — Consolidated

The Federal Reserve evaluates capital of a holding company with regard to the volume and risk of the operations of the consolidated corporation. It is the holding company's capital on a consolidated basis that the Federal Reserve believes must serve as the ultimate source of support and strength to the entire corporation.

For an examiner to consider capital adequate, holding company capital must:

- Support the volume and risk characteristics of all parent and subsidiary activities;

- Provide a sufficient cushion to absorb unanticipated losses arising from holding company and subsidiary activities;

- Support the level and composition of corporate and subsidiary borrowing; and

- Serve as a source of strength by providing an adequate base for the growth of risk assets and permitting entry into the capital markets as the need arises.

An essential step in the analysis of capital is the assessment of the risk characteristics and capital requirements deriving from the lending activities and operations of the parent and each of the operating subsidiaries.

Examiners will review capital based on these considerations:

33. The relationship of consolidated capital to consolidated assets as reflected in the ratio of primary capital to consolidated assets and the ratio of total capital to consolidated assets;

34. The capital requirements that derive from the asset quality and risk associated with each holding company activity;

35. The relationship of consolidated debt to primary capital;

36. The extent the company relies on long-term debt for its capital;

37. The extent the parent uses debt to fund capital investments in subsidiaries;

38. The trends of indices of capital adequacy and peer group ratio comparisons;

39. The management's ability to devise adequate capital plans and retention policies to correct any capital deficiency or planned expansion of risk assets;

40. The company's capacity to enter capital markets or tap other sources of long-term debt and equity;

41. The extent of any balance sheet concentration in any category or related categories of intangible assets, particularly those in excess of the 25 percent threshold, including the reasonableness of the amortization periods of those assets;

42. The relationship of high or inordinate off-balance sheet exposure to primary capital; and

43. Whether the BHC's consolidated capital position at least equals the sum of the capital requirements of the bank and nonbank subsidiaries as well as those of the parent company.

While the Federal Reserve will apply the ratio guidelines to both the bank and its holding company, the agency believes it is the consolidated entity's financial condition and strength that will ultimately determine the condition of the banking organization. To some extent strong consolidated holding company capital positions may offset minor deficiencies in the bank subsidiaries. However, bank capital positions, particularly those that reflect double leveraging, generally do not alleviate consolidated holding company capital deficiencies.

Regulators expect that banks and holding companies will satisfy both the minimum primary and total capital requirements. While both measures are important, the minimum level of primary capital to total assets is the critical first test of an institution's compliance with the guidelines. In meeting the total capital guidelines, examiners may consider secondary components of capital. However, an organization should not unduly rely on secondary components of capital simply to meet the total capital requirements, especially when conditions do not warrant additional debt. Any reliance on or issuance of debt or limited-life preferred stock to augment total capital should be consistent with the institution's overall financial condition and the general factors that are weighed in approving subordinated debt issues.

Strong primary capital positions may to some degree offset somewhat low total capital positions. Generally, however, primary capital positions below guideline minimums cannot be offset by higher total capital ratios.

The capital adequacy guidelines establish rating benchmarks for consolidated capital in the BOPEC system. While the capital guidelines will apply to the rating systems, ratings will continue to be a function of all the relevant objective and qualitative factors affecting an institution's financial condition that are set forth in the rating systems.

The Federal Reserve rates holding company capital in Zones and the BOPEC capital ratings are tied to those Zones. Primary capital ratios exceeding the guideline minimum and total capital ratios in Zone 1 will justify capital ratings in the BOPEC analysis of 1 (strong) or 2 (satisfactory), depending upon the value of the ratios and provided asset quality is on balance satisfactory for a capital rating of 1 or fair for a capital rating of 2.

A total capital ratio in Zone 2 generally indicates a BOPEC analysis capital rating of 3 (fair) or possibly 4 (marginal). The latter rating is more likely in the event that the primary capital ratio is below the minimum guideline ratio or if low total capital ratios are combined with serious asset problems. Institutions in Zone 2 with particularly strong primary ratios may qualify for satisfactory capital ratings, depending upon the level of the total capital ratio and overall asset quality.

Total capital ratios in Zone 3 or primary ratios below the minimum level imply capital ratings of 3 (fair), 4 (marginal), or possibly 5. Institutions in Zone 3 with primary ratios above the minimum may qualify for a rating of 3, provided asset quality is at least satisfactory. Primary ratios below the minimum or low total capital ratios combined with severe asset problems suggest ratings of 4 or 5. While high primary ratios may to some degree offset deficiencies in total capital ratios, high total capital ratios will not generally offset primary ratios below minimum acceptable levels.

Regulatory Risk: the Silent "R"

Consistent with the greater emphasis given to risk management in Federal Reserve examinations and supervisory policy statements, the BOPEC rating system has been revised to include a new risk management component similar to the new "S" component in the modified CAMELS rating system. Since 1996, examiners assign a formal supervisory rating to the adequacy of a holding company's risk management processes, including its internal controls. This step is a natural extension of current procedures that incorporate an assessment of risk management and internal controls during each on-site, full-scope examination.

The new risk management rating is a significant factor examiners consider when evaluating management under the BOPEC rating system. Examiners place primary consideration on findings relating to the following four elements of a sound risk management system:

- Active board and management oversight;

- Adequate policies, procedures, and limits;

- Accurate and independent measurement procedures and assessments of risk; and

- Strong internal controls.

A greater focus on risk management does not, of course, diminish the importance of reviewing capital adequacy, asset quality, earnings, liquidity, and other areas relevant to the evaluation of safety and soundness. Rather, the rating of the risk management process will bring together and summarize much of the analysis and many of the findings regarding an institution's process for managing and controlling risks. The formal rating is intended to highlight and incorporate both the quantitative and qualitative aspects of an examiner's review of an institution's overall process for identifying, measuring, monitoring, and controlling risk and to facilitate appropriate follow-up action.

Adequate risk management programs vary considerably in sophistication, depending on the size and complexity of the banking organization and the level of risk that it accepts. While all bank holding companies should be able to assess the major risks of the consolidated organization, parent companies that centrally manage the operations and functions of their subsidiary should have in place more comprehensive, detailed, and developed risk management systems than companies that delegate the management of risks to relatively autonomous banking subsidiaries.

Large, multinational organizations require far more elaborate and formal risk management systems in order to address their broader and typically more complex range of financial activities and to provide senior managers and directors with the information they need to monitor and direct day-to-day activities. For smaller institutions engaged solely in traditional banking activities and whose senior managers and directors are actively involved in the details of day-to-day operations, relatively basic risk management systems may be adequate.

Like the other BOPEC components, the risk management rating is based on a five-point numeric scale. This rating reflects findings within all four elements of sound risk management mentioned above and is reflected in the examiner's overall rating of management.

A rating of 1 indicates that management effectively identifies and controls all major types of risk posed by the institution's activities, including those from new products and changing market conditions. The board and management actively participate in monitoring and managing risk and ensure that appropriate policies and limits exist, and the board understands, reviews, and approves them. Policies and limits are supported by risk monitoring procedures, reports, and management information systems that provide necessary information and analysis to make timely and appropriate responses to changing conditions. Internal controls and audit procedures are sufficiently comprehensive and appropriate to the size and activities of the institution.

A 2-rating indicates that management of risk is largely effective, but lacking to some modest degree. While minor risk management weaknesses exist, these problems have been recognized and are being addressed. Overall, board and senior management's oversight policies and limits, risk monitoring procedures, reports, and management information systems are considered satisfactory and effective in maintaining a safe and sound institution. Generally, risks are being controlled in a manner that does not require additional or more than normal supervisory attention.

A 3-rating signifies risk management practices that are lacking in some important ways and, therefore, are a cause for more than normal supervisory attention. One or more of the four elements of sound risk management are considered fair, and have precluded the institution from fully addressing a significant risk to its operations. Certain risk management practices are in need of improvement to ensure that management and the board are able to identify, monitor, and control adequately all significant risks to the institution.

A 4-rating represents marginal risk management practices that generally fail to identify, monitor, and control significant risk exposures in many material respects. Generally, such a situation reflects a lack of adequate guidance and supervision by management and the board. One or more of the four elements of sound risk management are considered marginal and require immediate and concerted corrective action by the board and management. Deficiencies warrant a high degree of supervisory attention. Unless properly addressed, these conditions may result in unreliable financial records or reports or operating losses that could seriously affect the safety and soundness of the institution.

A 5-rating indicates a critical absence of effective risk management practices to identify, monitor, or control significant risk exposures. One or more of the four elements of sound risk management are considered wholly deficient and management and the board have not demonstrated the capability to address deficiencies. An immediate concern exists about the reliability of accounting records and regulatory reports and about potential losses that could result if management does not take corrective measures immediately. Deficiencies in risk management procedures and internal controls require immediate and close supervisory attention.

The Consumer Compliance Rating System

Overview

Under the uniform system adopted by the members of the FFIEC, each institution is assigned a consumer compliance rating evaluating both its compliance with consumer protection and civil rights statutes as well as the adequacy of its operating systems. Examiners follow the five-point scale in rating institutions in increasing order of supervisory concern. The rating reflects the regulators' evaluation of these factors:

- The nature and extent of present compliance with consumer protection and civil rights statutes and regulations;

- The commitment of management to compliance and its ability and willingness to assure continuing compliance; and

- The adequacy of operating systems, including internal procedures, controls, and audit activities designed to ensure compliance on a routine and consistent basis.

The FFIEC designed the rating system to help identify institutions whose compliance with consumer protection and civil rights statutes and regulations display weaknesses requiring special supervisory attention. Thus, the rating system is designed to identify an initial category of institutions that have compliance deficiencies warranting more than normal supervisory attention. These institutions do not present a significant risk of financial or other harm to consumers but do require more than the usual attention and are therefore assigned a 3 rating.

The rating system also identifies certain institutions whose weaknesses are so severe as to represent a substantial or general disregard for the law. Those institutions, depending on the nature and degree of their weaknesses, receive a rating of 4 or 5.

Consumer Compliance Composite Ratings

The consumer compliance composite ratings are defined as follows:

Composite 1

An institution in this category is in a strong compliance position. Management is capable of and staff is sufficient for effectuating compliance. An effective compliance program, including an efficient system of internal procedures, and controls, has been established. The institution promptly changes policies, procedures and compliance training to reflect changes in consumer statutes and regulations. The institution provides adequate training for its employees. If an examiner notes any violations, they relate to relatively minor deficiencies in forms or practices that are easily corrected. There is no evidence of discriminatory acts or practices, reimbursable violations, or practices resulting in repeat violations. Management promptly corrects violations and deficiencies. As a result, the institution gives no cause for supervisory concern.

Composite 2

An institution in this category is in a generally strong compliance position. Management is capable of administering an effective compliance program. Although the institution has established a system of internal operating procedures and controls to ensure compliance, violations have nonetheless occurred. Those violations, however, involve technical aspects of the law or result from oversight on the part of operating personnel. Modification in the bank's compliance program or the establishment of additional review or audit procedures may eliminate many of the violations. Compliance training is satisfactory. There is no evidence of discriminatory acts or practices, reimbursable violations, or practices resulting in repeat violations.

Composite 3

Generally, an institution in this category is in a less than satisfactory compliance position and requires more than normal supervision to remedy deficiencies. Violations may be numerous. In addition, previously identified practices resulting in violations may remain uncorrected. Overcharges, if present, involve a few consumers and are minimal in amount. There is no evidence of discriminatory acts or practices.

Although management may have the ability to comply with the law and regulations, increased efforts are necessary. The numerous violations indicate that management has not devoted sufficient time and attention to consumer compliance. Operating procedures and controls have not proven effective and require strengthening by, among other things, designating a compliance officer and developing and implementing a comprehensive and effective compliance program. By identifying such an institution early, the regulator may employ additional supervisory measures to eliminate violations and prevent further deterioration in the institution's less than satisfactory compliance position.

Composite 4

An institution in this category requires close supervisory attention and monitoring to promptly correct the serious compliance problems disclosed. Numerous violations are present. Overcharges, if any, affect a significant number of consumers and involve a substantial amount of money. Often practices resulting in violations and cited at previous examinations remain uncorrected. Discriminatory acts or practices may be in evidence. Clearly, management has not exerted sufficient effort to ensure compliance. Its attitude may indicate a lack of interest in administering an effective compliance program that may have contributed to the seriousness of the institution's compliance problems. Internal procedures and controls have not proven effective and are seriously deficient. Prompt action on the part of the supervisory agency may enable the institution to correct its deficiencies and improve its compliance position.

Composite 5

An institution in this category is in need of the strongest supervisory attention and monitoring. It is substantially in noncompliance with the consumer statutes and regulations. Management has demonstrated its unwillingness or inability to operate within the scope of consumer statutes and regulation. Previous efforts on the part of the regulatory authority to obtain voluntary compliance have been unproductive. Discrimination, substantial overcharges, or practices resulting in serious repeat violations are present.

The FDIC's MVP Rating Scheme

While the FDIC follows the uniform FFIEC rating system, that agency has adopted a three-component rating system to assist examiners in arriving at a composite rating for consumer compliance.

Using the five-point scale the FDIC examiners rate:

- Management — elements include attitude toward consumer compliance, quality of oversight, and effort to comply;

- Violations — elements include repeat violations, reimbursable violations, and violations involving apparent discrimination; and

- Program — examiners consider the effectiveness of the institution's compliance program.

The Uniform Interagency Rating System for Data Processing Organizations

Financial institution regulators increasingly view adequate information systems as essential for a financial institution's risk management program. Information systems can affect an institution's control of almost all of the risks that the regulators identify in their supervision by risk programs. Because of this growing importance in risk management, we discuss at length in a following section of this *Handbook* the methods and expectations of the regulators in conducting data processing examinations. In this section we discuss the ratings that result from those examinations.

The rating system for data processing operations is similar to the UFIRS in which examiners rate the overall condition of a financial institution. In evaluating the electronic data processing (EDP) systems of a financial institution, regulators will review four critical functions of a data processing organization:

- Audit;

- Management;

- System development and programming; and
- Computer operations.

Regulators assign each data processing organization a composite rating based upon their separate performance ratings assigned to the four functions.

The composite rating and each performance rating use the five-point scale in descending order of quality of performance. To arrive at a composite rating, examiners must consider the interrelationships and relative importance of the four functions to the organization. Occasionally, the examiners will find factors that are not reflected in any specific performance rating but are important to the organization's overall condition and should be reflected in the composite rating.

Audit

In reviewing EDP operations, examiners will rate audit on the five-point scale with respect to:

- Organization:
    - Independence;
    - Board of directors' support;
    - Resources allocated; and
    - Management and staff succession.
- Staff Qualifications Training
- Quality, scope, and frequency of audits:
    - Standards and procedures provide for adequate audits;
    - Compliance;
    - Follow-up and correction of exceptions;
    - Working papers and documentation;
    - Use, effectiveness, and documentation of audit software; and
    - Audit reports.

Management

Examiners will rate management on the five-point scale according to these considerations:

- Organization:

    - Resources allocated to EDP operations;

    - Leadership;

    - Administrative abilities;

    - Qualifications;

    - Delegation of responsibility;

    - Support; and

    - Management succession.

- Correction of deficiencies

- Laws and Regulations:

    - Awareness of requirements;

    - Compliance; and

    - Contracts.

- Planning:

    - Risk analysis in the planning process;

    - User involvement;

    - Senior management involvement; and

    - Budget.

- Development and enforcement of effective and appropriate standards and procedures

- Development and enforcement of appropriate internal controls

- Development and enforcement of and appropriate physical security program

- Financial condition

Systems and Programming

Examiners rate systems and programming on the five-point scale considering these factors:

- Organization:

    - Separation of duties;

    - Resources allocated; and

    - Management and staff succession.

- Qualifications and training of staff

- Adequacy of and compliance with appropriate standards and procedures

- Documentation:

    - Completeness;

    - Organization; and

    - Storage and security.

- Internal Controls:

    - Modification and change procedures;

    - Documentation and implementation of authorizations; and

    - Program library maintenance, including systems development.

- Physical Security:

    - Documentation;

    - Software; and

    - On-line systems.

Computer Operations

Examiners will rate computer operations considering these factors:

- Organization:

    – Separation of duties;

    – Resources allocated; and

    – Management and staffing succession.

- The qualifications and training of staff

- Standards and Procedures:

    – Adequacy;

    – Compliance; and

    – User liaison.

- Operations:

    – Data entry control;

    – Processing controls;

    – Output distribution controls;

    – Physical security;

    – Emergency plans; and

    – User communication.

The Off-Site Rating Systems — SEER and NBSS

For the rating systems discussed above, examiners will conduct an on-site visit to the institution. Their ratings will depend on actual observation of the financial records of the institution and a direct review of files, practices, policies, and procedures. The examination process is an extremely detailed one that occurs in most institutions no more than once each year.

The examination process is a snapshot of the state of the financial institution at a certain time. In order to be more aware of changing conditions in certain financial institutions, the regulators have created off-site methods of evaluating an institution's condition. The material they review comes from the quarterly call reports financial institutions must file with their federal regulator and from other required regulatory reports.

The Comptroller of the Currency devised the National Bank Surveillance System ("NBSS") in the mid-1970s as an early warning system to detect problem banks or potential problem banks. The NBSS relies on a comprehensive ratio analysis using call report figures and a comparison against peer group results. The OCC also requires examiners on site to reach some overall conclusions about the bank's future prospects to add information to the NBSS database.

The Federal Reserve and the FDIC followed with similar analytical systems — the Uniform Bank Surveillance Screen ("UBSS") and CAEL (four of the six CAMELS components), respectively. More recently the Federal Reserve created the SEER (Systems to Estimate Examination Ratings) system to replace the UBSS. All three agencies use their systems to monitor the financial condition of supervised institutions between examinations and inspections.

The off-site systems identify outliers in the industry based on poor peer group rankings or their failure to meet levels of certain ratios that the agencies have established as benchmarks. The agencies use ratio analysis and econometric models to project an institution's rating in the quarters between examinations or inspections. The advantage for regulators is that the off-site reviews are based on newer data than the CAMELS ratings. A disadvantage is that the methods of analysis still produce inaccurate projections of institution's ratings 10 percent or more of the time.

The agencies continue to make improvements in their off-site reviews, and the latest systems are more accurate predictors of risk than the earlier. With improved off-site reviews, the agencies can achieve two goals. They can intervene earlier in a problem institution in order to protect the banking system and the deposit insurance fund. They can also use financial and regulatory resources more efficiently, ultimately reducing the cost of regulation to the financial institutions they supervise.

IX. Regulatory Enforcement

Introduction 178

Informal Remedies 178

Formal Remedies 178

License Revocations 185

Introduction

Most disagreements between a financial institution and its regulators are resolved through discussion or other informal means. When informal resolution fails, the regulator possesses a powerful array of enforcement powers to employ against what the regulator believes to be an unsafe or unsound banking practice or a violation of law. These powers include cease-and-desist orders, removal of officers and directors, civil money penalties, and — ultimately — franchise termination.

Informal Remedies

Bank regulators routinely monitor the condition of each bank, savings association, bank holding company, and foreign bank branch or agency through off-site surveillance and on-site inspections or examinations. The regulators communicate the results of this monitoring to each supervised institution through correspondence, informal discussions, meetings with management and directors, and examination reports. This communication includes (as explained elsewhere) an overall numerical or other rating at the end of each inspection or examination.

A bank or holding company's managers and directors, thus, usually are well aware of how their regulators view the institution and of any issues that may cause regulatory concern. They typically discuss these concerns with the regulators and informally reach an understanding about what, if any, action the institution will take to address these concerns. This understanding often is reflected in the examination or inspection report or in correspondence with the regulator. A regulator who wants to emphasize the seriousness of a particular concern may ask the institution's board of directors to sign a memorandum of understanding specifying the remedial actions to be taken.

Regulators also consider the results of their supervisory monitoring when acting on an institution's application to expand or to undertake a new activity. The regulator may instruct the institution to file no applications or may deny any applications that are filed, pending correction of the perceived regulatory problem. Holding a bank's strategic plans hostage in this manner is an extremely effective, if informal, regulatory remedy.

Formal Remedies

A federal regulator (e.g., OCC, FRB, FDIC, and OTS) may invoke a formal administrative remedy against:

- An FDIC-insured bank;

- An FDIC-insured savings association;
- A bank holding company or its nonbank subsidiaries;
- A foreign bank's U.S. branch, agency, commercial lending company, or nonbank subsidiary; and
- An "institution-affiliated party" of any of the above.

One type of formal remedy — civil money penalties — also may be imposed against a savings association's holding company.

An "institution-affiliated party" includes an officer, director, employee, or controlling shareholder, or other person participating in an entity's affairs. In some instances, an outside contractor, such as an appraiser, accountant, or attorney, may be an institution-affiliated party, and, thus, subject to these formal remedies.

While the procedures vary, each formal remedy requires:

- Notice;
- An opportunity to respond and submit facts and arguments against the proposed regulatory action;
- A written agency decision and order; and
- An opportunity for some degree of review by a federal court.

Although this discussion is limited to the federal regulators, many state regulators have similar powers.

Cease-and-Desist Orders

A federal regulator may charge any FDIC-insured depository, a bank holding company, a foreign bank branch or agency, or an institution-affiliated party with engaging in an unsafe or unsound banking practice or a violation of law. After proving those charges in a formal, public proceeding before an administrative law judge (ALJ), the regulator may order the person or entity charged to cease and desist from the unsafe or unsound practice or the violation of law. The order also may direct affirmative action to correct conditions resulting from the challenged conduct.

The specific provisions of a cease-and-desist order are first recommended by the ALJ who presides at the evidentiary hearing. That recommended order becomes the regulatory agency's final order, unless a party to the proceeding asks the agency head to review the ALJ's recommended decision and order. The agency head may accept, reject, or rewrite the ALJ's recommended order.

When the agency's administrative proceeding is complete and its cease-and-desist order is final, a party subject to the order may seek review in a federal court of appeals. The court does not, itself, take any new evidence, but instead determines whether — based on the record before the regulatory agency — the regulator's order is supported by substantial evidence and otherwise in accordance with law.

A final cease and desist order is enforceable through the federal courts. In addition, failure to comply with the order can result in heavy civil money penalties.

Temporary Cease-and-Desist Orders

A federal regulator who believes that an uncorrected unsafe or unsound practice or violation of law may endanger an insured depository or its depositors before completion of a formal cease-and-desist proceeding may begin that proceeding with both a notice of charges and a temporary order. The temporary order, like a permanent one, may direct the taking of affirmative corrective actions.

A temporary cease-and-desist order is immediately effective and continues until the underlying cease-and-desist proceeding is completed. A bank or other party who is served with a temporary order may, within 10 days, ask a federal district court to overturn the order. The court in this instance is not limited to an administrative record, since none exists, but instead receives evidence directly from the regulator and from the other parties to the proceeding.

A temporary order, like a permanent one, is enforceable both through the federal courts and by the assessment of civil money penalties.

Removal of Institution-Affiliated Parties

A federal regulator may remove from office an "institution-affiliated party" whose conduct meets three criteria:

- It violates a law, cease-and-desist order, or other enforceable regulatory condition, constitutes an unsafe or unsound banking practice, or breaches a fiduciary duty;

- It results in damage to the institution, prejudice to its depositors, or financial gain to the affiliated party; and

- It involves personal dishonesty or demonstrates willful and continuing disregard for the institution's safety and soundness.

The removal proceeding, like a cease-and-desist proceeding, is initiated by a notice written by the regulator and is tried before an ALJ who issues a recommended decision that is subject to review by the head of the regulatory agency. In the case of a national bank, the final decision is made by the Federal Reserve Board rather than the Comptroller of the Currency. The final decision is subject to review on the administrative record by a federal court of appeals.

A regulator may suspend an institution-affiliated party while the removal proceeding is pending if the regulator determines that doing so is necessary to protect the depository institution or its depositors. Within 10 days after receiving a suspension order, the person who is suspended may ask a federal district court to overturn it. The court in this instance receives directly whatever evidence it needs to make its decision.

A regulator also may suspend an institution-affiliated party who has been charged either with a felony involving dishonesty or breach of trust or with a violation of federal anti-money-laundering laws. To do so, the regulator must find that keeping the person in office during the pendency of the felony charges may threaten the interest of depositors or impair public confidence in the institution. The suspension lasts until criminal proceedings are completed.

If the person is convicted, then the agency may order his or her permanent removal from the institution and must order permanent removal for a money-laundering conviction.

A person who is suspended or removed under these provisions may request an informal hearing before the regulatory agency for the limited purpose of contending that his or her continuation in office does not threaten the interest of depositors or impair public confidence in the institution.

A suspension or removal order is industry-wide. The person to whom it is directed is barred not only from his or her own institution, but also from participating in the affairs of any insured depository, any bank holding company, any farm credit bank, or any federal bank regulatory agency. Forbidden activities include serving as an officer, employee, or director or in any other capacity as an institution-affiliated party; soliciting or voting proxies; or voting for a director.

Suspension or removal orders are enforceable through the federal courts. In addition, failure to comply with a suspension or removal order can result in heavy civil money penalties. Finally, violation of a suspension or removal order is a federal crime carrying a maximum penalty of a $1-million fine and five years' imprisonment.

Civil Money Penalties — in General

A regulator may assess a civil money penalty of up to $5,000 per day against an FDIC-insured depository, a bank holding company, a foreign bank branch or agency, or an institution-affiliated party for violating:

- A statute or regulation;

- A temporary or final cease-and-desist order;

- A suspension or removal order;

- An order concerning capital issued under the prompt corrective action provisions;

- A condition imposed in writing by the regulator when granting an application; and

- A written agreement between the institution and the agency.

The maximum penalty increases to $25,000 per day for such a violation, or for recklessly engaging in an unsafe or unsound banking practice, or for a breach of fiduciary duty, if the violation, practice, or breach:

- Is part of a pattern or practice of misconduct;

- Exposes the depository institution to the likelihood of more than a minimal loss; and

- Results in a financial benefit or gain to the party being penalized.

The maximum fine increases to a total of $1 million if the violation, practice, or breach was knowing and knowingly caused either a substantial loss to the institution or a substantial gain to the assessed party. If the fine is being assessed against an insured depository, then the maximum cannot exceed 1 percent of its total assets.

A regulator assesses a civil money penalty by sending a notice stating the penalty proposed and the reasons for it. The party receiving the notice may request a formal hearing before an ALJ. The ALJ will receive evidence about the reasons for assessing the penalty and about any mitigating factors. Mitigating factors include:

- The financial resources and good faith of the party assessed.

- The gravity of the violation.

- The history of previous violations.

- Others matters as justice may require.

As with cease-and-desist proceedings, the ALJ issues a recommended decision and assessment order. Any party to the proceeding may ask the agency head to review and modify the ALJ's decision. The final decision by the head of the agency may be appealed to a federal court of appeals for review based on the administrative record.

The regulator may file an action in federal district court to collect any unpaid penalty. The district court does not have authority to review the appropriateness of the penalty assessed.

Civil Money Penalties — Reports

A bank regulator may assess a civil money penalty of up to $20,000 per day against any bank that fails to file its quarterly Report of Condition and Income (Call Report) or files a report containing false or misleading information.

The bank may reduce the maximum penalty to $2,000 per day by showing that the report was minimally late through inadvertent error or that the failure to file or the inclusion of false or misleading information was an inadvertent error that occurred despite maintaining procedures reasonably adapted to prevent such a mistake. If, on the other hand, the error was knowing or reckless, then the maximum penalty increases to $1 million, but not to exceed 1 percent of the bank's total assets. Identical civil money penalties apply to the reports that:

- A savings association must file with OTS;

- A bank holding company must file with the Federal Reserve; and

- A savings and loan holding company must file with OTS.

The procedures for assessing, contesting, and collecting these reporting penalties are the same as described above for other civil money penalties.

Civil Money Penalties — Holding Companies

The Federal Reserve may assess a civil money penalty of up to $25,000 per day against any company that violates the Bank Holding Company Act or any regulation or order issued under that Act. OTS may assess a similar penalty against any company that violates the Savings and Loan Holding Company Act or a regulation or order issued under that Act. There is no maximum penalty.

The procedures for assessing, contesting, and collecting these holding company penalties are the same as those for other civil money penalties.

Criminal penalties also apply to violations of the Bank Holding Company Act or the Savings and Loan Holding Company Act. A knowing violation of one of these acts or an order or regulation issued under them may be punished by a fine of $100,000 per day and imprisonment of one year. A knowing violation with the intent to deceive, defraud, or profit significantly may be punished by a fine of $1 million per day and five years imprisonment.

Insurance Termination

FDIC may terminate the insurance for the depositors of any bank or savings association. The reasons for doing so include:

- The institution or its directors are engaging in unsafe or unsound banking practices;

- The institution is in an unsafe or unsound condition; and

- The institution or its directors have violated any applicable statute, regulation, order, or regulatory condition.

FDIC begins an insurance termination proceeding by notifying the institution's primary federal or state regulator of the reasons FDIC wishes to revoke the entity's insurance. If the condition causing FDIC's concern is not corrected within 30 days, FDIC then may serve the institution with a notice of charges on which FDIC intends to terminate its insurance.

The bank then is entitled to the same procedures as in a cease-and-desist proceeding: a formal evidentiary hearing before an ALJ, a recommended ALJ decision, review of that decision by FDIC's board of directors, and review of the FDIC's final decision by a federal court of appeals based on the administrative record. FDIC may use a temporary order to suspend deposit insurance or other means to shorten the time frame for revoking insurance.

A bank or savings association whose insurance is terminated must notify each of its depositors. Existing deposits remain temporarily insured for a period specified by FDIC of at least six months, but not longer than two years. Any new or additional deposits during this temporary period are not insured.

License Revocations

In extreme cases, a regulator will seize a bank or revoke its license to conduct a banking business or both. Ways this may happen include the following:

Receivership

The OCC may appoint the FDIC to be the receiver of a national bank whenever the OCC determines that:

- The bank's liabilities exceed its assets;

- An unsafe or unsound practice or a violation of law is causing a substantial dissipation of the bank's assets or earnings, or is likely to weaken the condition of the institution or otherwise prejudice the interest of depositors;

- The bank is unlikely to be able to pay its obligations in the normal course of business;

- The bank has insufficient capital, is likely to incur losses that will deplete substantially all of its capital, or otherwise is in an unsafe or unsound condition to transact banking business;

- The bank willfully has violated a cease-and-desist order;

- The bank has fewer than five directors; and

- The bank has concealed its books or records or has refused to make them available for examination.

OCC's appointment of a receiver is not subject to review or oversight by any court or any other authority. OTS's appointment of a receiver is subject to challenge in a federal district court. OTS for the same reasons may appoint FDIC to be receiver of a federal savings association.

The laws of most states invest similar authority in a state bank regulatory official to appoint a receiver (usually the FDIC) for a state bank or savings association. The laws of some states permit a state court to either approve or review the determination to appoint a receiver. The FDIC may appoint itself as receiver of an insured state bank or savings association if it determines the state institution meets one or more of the grounds for appointing a national bank receiver.

The FDIC, acting as receiver, seizes the bank, provides for the payment of insured depositors, and liquidates the bank's assets for the benefit of its creditors (including FDIC as subrogee of the insured depositors whom it has paid). Often the majority of the failed bank's assets and its deposit liabilities are transferred in bulk to another, healthy bank. Bank shareholders usually receive nothing.

Conservatorship

When conditions exist at a national bank that would permit appointment of a receiver, OCC may appoint a conservator instead. OTS similarly may appoint a conservator for a federal savings association.

The conservator seizes the bank or savings association and exercises all the powers of its directors and stockholders. The bank or savings association may sue in federal court to terminate the appointment of a conservator.

Conservators are rarely appointed. Sometimes, however, they can serve a special purpose, such as acting quickly in place of the shareholders to approve a bulk sale of the assets and liabilities to another bank who is willing to take over the business of a troubled institution without the financial assistance of an FDIC receivership.

Many states also provide for the appointment of a conservator for a state bank.

Termination of Foreign Bank Offices

The OCC may terminate the license of a federal branch or agency of a foreign bank if the bank violates the International Banking Act or any order issued by OCC under that act, or if a conservator or receiver has been appointed for the foreign bank's head office. OCC must give the foreign bank notice and an opportunity for a hearing. OCC may deny a hearing if OCC determines that a hearing would not be in the public interest.

The Federal Reserve may terminate the state branch or agency if the Fed determines:

- The foreign bank is not subjected by its home country to comprehensive supervision on a consolidated basis.

- The bank has committed, in the United States, a violation of law or engaged in an unsafe or unsound banking practice, and, as a result, the Fed finds that continued operation of the state branch or agency would be inconsistent with the public interest or with U.S. banking law.

The Fed, for these same reasons, may recommend to OCC that it revoke the license of a federal branch or agency.

The Fed has stated that lack of comprehensive consolidated home country supervision would not, by itself, be sufficient reason for terminating the activities of a foreign bank's state branch or agency. The Fed must give notice of a proposed termination both to the foreign bank and to the state supervisor of the branch or agency involved. It also must provide the foreign bank a hearing, unless the Fed determines that expeditious action is required to protect the public interest.

A foreign bank may ask a federal court of appeals to review either an OCC or a Fed order to close a branch or agency. The court does not itself take any new evidence, but instead determines whether — based on the record before the regulatory agency — the regulator's order is supported by substantial evidence and otherwise in accordance with law.

The order to close a foreign bank's branch or agency is enforceable through a federal district court.

X. U.S. Sentencing Guidelines

Introduction and Purpose 190

The Importance of an Effective Compliance Program 190

Introduction and Purpose

The U.S. Sentencing Commission issued the Guidelines for Sentencing Organizations ("Sentencing Guidelines" or "Guidelines") in November 1992. These Guidelines govern federal judges in determining the severity of the penalty imposed on a corporation — such as a bank — that has been found guilty of a federal crime.

The Importance of an Effective Compliance Program

Under U.S. law, a bank may be liable for criminal acts of an employee acting in the course of corporate employment. Even if an employee did not have the requisite intent to commit a crime, a bank may be criminally liable if a jury finds that it *should have known* of the violation through the combined knowledge of its employees.

According to the Sentencing Commission, preventive measures by corporate management can significantly reduce the likelihood and impact of corporate crime. Thus, the Guidelines require a judge imposing a fine on a bank to consider as a mitigating factor the existence of "an effective compliance program to prevent and detect violations of law."

An effective compliance program can diminish the threat of criminal prosecution. In the event of prosecution, the presence of an effective compliance program can reduce the fine by as much as 60 percent. Conversely, management tolerance of, or participation in, criminal activity is an aggravating factor that will require substantially increased penalties.

Elements of an Effective Compliance Program

The Guidelines emphasize that the compliance program must be appropriate to the size of the organization and tailored to the kinds of risks inherent in its particular business activities. The larger the organization, the more formal the program should be.

Under the Guidelines, an effective compliance program should:

1. Assign high-level personnel overall responsibility for overseeing compliance standards and procedures.

2. Establish for its employees and agents compliance standards and procedures capable of reducing the prospect of criminal conduct.

3. Communicate standards and procedures to all employees and other agents through required participation in training programs or distribution of publications with practical explanations of compliance requirements.

4. Use monitoring and auditing systems designed to detect criminal conduct by employees and agents.

5. Enforce bank standards through appropriate disciplinary mechanisms, including discipline of individuals responsible for failure to detect an offense.

6. Use due care not to delegate substantial discretionary authority to individuals whom the bank knows or should know (through due diligence) have a propensity to engage in illegal activities.

7. Establish and publicize a reporting system for employees and agents to report criminal conduct by others in the organization without fear of retribution.

8. Take all reasonable steps to respond to an offense once it has been detected. Those steps include actions to prevent further similar offenses, including necessary modifications to its program to prevent and detect violations of law.

These steps are not all-inclusive. The Commission expects a bank to use a reasonable degree of ingenuity to devise a compliance program that actually works. An effective compliance program cannot detect all offenses — including the offense for which the bank may be sentenced — but it must be constructed to show that the bank has been diligent in trying to prevent its employees and agents from engaging in criminal conduct.

Range of Penalties

The Sentencing Guidelines permit a sentencing judge to place a bank on probation for one to five years. A bank also may be ordered to compensate identifiable victims — either monetarily or through community service — for their losses. Most commonly, a sentencing judge will impose a fine on a bank. Depending on the offense and any aggravating or mitigating factors, a fine against a bank may range from $5,000 to 1 percent of its assets.

Voluntary Disclosure

One of the most important mitigating factors under the Sentencing Guidelines is the voluntary disclosure by the bank of any possible violations of law. Voluntary disclosure significantly reduces a bank's risk of criminal prosecution, and — if prosecution occurs — mitigates the severity of any resulting penalties.

Under the guidelines, a bank should:

- Report the offense to the proper government authorities prior to an imminent threat of disclosure or government investigation, and within a reasonably prompt time after becoming aware of the offense;

- Cooperate fully in the investigation; and

- Demonstrate recognition and affirmative acceptance of responsibility for the criminal conduct.

Internal Reporting Systems

Essential to the process of voluntary disclosure is the existence of an internal reporting system. Employees must be able to report what they see or suspect to management without fear of retribution. Internal reporting systems — such as hotlines and ombudsmen — provide anonymity for employees and allow management to investigate allegations of illegal activity and report any such confirmed activity to the proper authorities.

XI. Interagency Safety and Soundness Guidelines

Introduction and Purpose 194

Operational and Managerial Standards 194

Agencies' Existing Authority 195

Compliance Plan 195

Enforcement 196

Introduction and Purpose

In July 1995, the federal banking agencies (the OCC, FRB, FDIC, and OTS) collectively adopted the Interagency Guidelines Establishing Standards for Safety and Soundness. Congress required this action in amendments to the Federal Deposit Insurance Act. The guidelines are designed to encourage the adoption of safe and sound banking practices appropriate to the size of the institution and the nature and scope of its activities. The guidelines consist of:

- Operational and managerial standards; and

- Compensation standards.

In August 1996, the agencies established standards relating to asset quality and earnings, thus completing the requirements of section 132 of the Federal Deposit Insurance Corporation Improvement Act of 1991.

Operation and Managerial Standards

Although the guidelines establish certain operational and managerial standards, they do not specify how an institution should achieve them. This flexibility allows the institution to use the method that is best suited to its size, nature, and scope of activities. An institution must meet the following operational and managerial standards:

Internal controls and information systems. An institution should have internal controls and information systems that provide clear lines of authority, effective risk assessment, and compliance with applicable laws. The design and execution of the controls should be tailored to the institution's operating environment.

Internal audit system. An institution should have an internal audit system with adequate testing and review of internal controls. A system of independent reviews may be used by an institution whose size and scope of operations does not warrant a full-scale system.

Loan documentation. An institution should establish loan documentation practices that provide for proper recording or perfection of the security interest. The documentation practices should permit different treatment according to loan type and amount.

Credit underwriting. An institution should act within the general parameters of safe and sound credit underwriting practices by evaluating the nature of the markets, the borrower, and the concentration of credit risk.

Interest rate exposure. An institution should manage interest rate risk in a manner appropriate to its size and the complexity of its assets and liabilities. The institution should establish procedures for periodic reports on risk management to the institution's management and board of directors.

Asset growth. An institution should base its asset growth on a plan that fully considers the source of the growth, the risks presented by the growth, and the effect of growth on capital. The regulatory agencies will evaluate asset growth against the institution's overall strategic plan for growth.

Compensation, fees, and benefits. An institution should maintain safeguards to assure that its compensation, fees, or benefits are not excessive and that payments will not lead to material financial loss. The agencies distinguish the requirement of safeguards from the separate standards governing the actual payment of excessive compensation, discussed below.

Asset quality. An institution should have monitoring and reporting systems to identify problem assets, prevent deterioration in those assets, and estimate inherent losses. Material concentrations of credit risk and the level of capital reserves should be considered when forming corrective action plans.

Earnings. An institution should evaluate earnings to ensure that they are sufficient to maintain adequate capital and reserves. Monitoring and reporting systems should be in place for prompt remedial action.

Agencies' Existing Authority

The provisions of this interagency rule merely provide guidance. The standards do not preclude any agency from using its criteria when determining the safety and soundness of an institution. An institution that complies with the guidelines may be found to be in unsafe or unsound condition or to have engaged in an unsafe or unsound practice under an agency's own rules. Conversely, failure to comply with the standards does not necessarily constitute an unsafe or unsound practice, except for failure to comply with the prohibition on compensation standard.

Compliance Plan

If an agency determines that an institution fails to meet any standard under the guidelines, then it may request that the institution file a written compliance plan. This plan should include:

- A description of the steps the institution will take to correct the deficiency; and

- The time within which those steps will be taken.

Within 30 days after an agency request, the institution must submit the compliance plan to the appropriate regulator for approval.

Enforcement

Failure to properly file or adhere to the compliance plan may subject the institution to various sanctions. The agency must, by order, require the institution to correct the deficiency. This order is enforceable in court and failure to comply with it could result in civil penalties. Agencies retain the authority to pursue other, more appropriate or effective courses of action for noncompliance. An agency may begin supervisory action against an institution even if it did not request the institution to file a compliance plan.

Index

A

Adverse report, 35
American Institute of Certified Public Accountants (AICPA), 32, 34
Audits
   compliance risk and, 22
   external
      adverse report, 35
      board of director responsibility, 31–32
      disclaimer report, 35
      fieldwork standards for, 33
      general standards for, 33
      independence in, 33–34
      information systems and, 57
      internal audit coordination, 30
      qualified report, 34–35
      reports for, 33, 34–35
      report standards for, 33
      standards for, 32–33
      unqualified report, 34
   internal
      charter for, 25–26
      compliance function and, 41–42
      documentation of, 29
      external audit coordination, 30
      follow-up for, 29–30
      frequency of, 26–27
      independence in, 26, 55
      information systems and, 55–57
      organization of, 28
      outsourcing in, 30–31
      planning of, 26
      reports for, 29
      scope of, 26–27
      supervision of, 28–29
      work program for, 27–28
   purpose of, 22
   references regarding, 35
   risk–based, 18–19, 20, 23–25
      policies/procedures for, 24
      written standards for, 24–25
   transaction risk and, 22
Automated clearing house (ACH), 96
Automated teller machines (ATMs), 94

B

Bank holding companies, 9
   geographic restrictions, 10
   securities activities, 10–11
Bank Holding Company Act, 183–84
Bank Insurance Fund (BIF), 6, 8
BOPEC rating system
   bank condition, 156–57
   capital adequacy, 162–65
   consolidated earnings, 160–62
   finances, 154
   management, 154–56
   nonbank condition, 157–59
   overview of, 122, 151–54
   parent company, 159–60
   risk management, 165–67
Branches, bank. **See** Foreign banks; Geographic restrictions
Business recovery planning (BRP), 85–91
   business impact analysis, 86
   cold site agreement, 87
   data file backup, 88–89
   disk mirroring, 89
   hot site agreement, 86–87
   plan development, 86, 90
   plan evaluation, 86, 90–91
   plan testing, 86, 90
   software backup, 87–88
   strategy options, 86–87
   telecommunications backup, 89–90

C

Cease–and–desist orders, 179–80
   temporary, 180
Certified Public Accountants (CPAs), 32–35
CHIPS, 91
Cold site agreement, 87
Combined rating system, 148
Commercial banks, 6
   geographic restrictions, 9–10
Community Reinvestment performance, 122
Compliance function
   Compliance Committee, 38
   Compliance Officer, 38

Compliance function *(continued)*
   internal audits and, 41–42
   operating management
      assistance for, 41
      oversight of, 40
      responsibility of, 40–41
      support for, 39
   personnel selection, 42
   personnel training, 42
      new personnel, 42–43
      senior management and, 42
   program goals, 38
   records
      establishment of, 43
      review of, 43–44
   risks, 15, 18–19
      audits and, 22
      management of, 44–45
      sentencing guidelines and, 190–91
   senior management
      personnel training and, 42
      responsibility of, 39–40
      support for, 38–39
Computer operations, 67–73
   duty separation/rotation, 68–69
   equipment control, 70
   equipment maintenance, 69–70
   library control, 71–72
   operator control, 71
   rating systems and, 174
   transaction processing, 72–73
   workload scheduling, 70
   See also End–user computing (EUC)
Consumer Compliance Rating System
   composite ratings, 168–70
   FDIC and, 170
   overview of, 122, 167–68
Credit risk, 15, 17, 19, 20, 92–93
Credit unions, 7

D

Database
   administrator for, 67
   monitoring of, 67
Data exchange, 118
Data file backup, 88–89
Data integrity
   computer virus control, 84–85
   output control, 81–82
   telecommunication control, 82
   transmission control, 83–84
   user education, 85
Data security, 66–67, 77–78
De novo branches, 10
Disclaimer report, 35
Disk mirroring, 89
Documentation
   information systems

Documentation *(continued)*
      manual documentation, 66
      program documentation, 61, 65–66
   internal audits, 29
   regulatory examination, 50
Document imaging, 106
Dual licensing system, 11

E

Eavesdropping, 83
Edge Act and Agreement Corporations, 11
Electronic funds transfer (EFT)
   automated clearing house (ACH), 96
   automated teller machines (ATMs), 94
   communication control, 94
   credit risk, 92–93
   insurance for, 100–101
   internal control, 98–101
   internet banking, 97–98
   nondeposit investment products, 98
   operational control, 93
   payment order origination, 91–92
   PINs, 95, 98–100
   point–of–sale (POS), 94–95
   retail, 94, 98–101
   risk control, 92
   smart cards, 95
   wholesale, 91
End–user computing (EUC)
   acquisition criteria, 102
   communications in, 105–6
   development of, 103–4
   existing inventory, 101–2
   security for, 102–3
   usage of, 104–5

F

Federal Deposit Insurance Corporation (FDIC)
   federal/state regulations and, 11–12
   rating systems and, 125, 146, 170, 175
   regulatory enforcement and, 184–86
   regulatory examination and, 48
   regulatory system and, 6, 7, 8, 11–12
   risk–focused examination and, 16–17
Federal Deposit Insurance Corporation Improvement Act (FDICIA) (1991), 22, 55
   rating systems and, 136–37
Federal Financial Institutions Examination Council (FFIEC), 48, 122, 125–26, 145–46, 167–68
Federal Home Loan Bank Board, 17, 125–26
Federal regulations, 11–12
Federal Reserve Banks, 9, 92, 96
Federal Reserve Board (FRB)
   rating systems and, 125, 146, 149–50, 151–54, 175
   regulatory examination and, 48
   regulatory system and, 8–9, 11
   risk–focused examination and, 16

Federal Reserve Board (FRB) *(continued)*
   year 2000 problem, 110–12
Federal Reserve System
   audits and, 30–31
   regulatory system and, 8–9, 11
Fedwire, 91
Financial Accounting Standards Board (FASB), 32
First Day Letter, 49
Foreign banks
   rating systems
      annual examination plan, 150–51
      Combined rating, 148
      ROCA, 122, 146–48, 150
      SOSA, 122, 149–50
   regulatory enforcement, 186–87
Foreign Bank Supervision Enhancement Act (1991), 146
Foreign exchange risk, 15

G

Generally accepted accounting principles (GAAP), 32, 34–35
Generally accepted auditing standards (GAAS), 32–33, 34–35
Geographic restrictions
   bank holding companies, 10
   commercial banks, 9–10
   de novo branches, 10
   Interstate Act (1994), 9–10
   opting–out, 9–10
   savings associations, 10
Glass–Steagall Act (1933), 10

H

Hot site agreement, 86–87

I

Independence (audits)
   external, 33–34
   internal, 26, 55
Information control, 51
Information systems
   business recovery planning (BRP), 85–91
      business impact analysis, 86
      cold site agreement, 87
      data file backup, 88–89
      disk mirroring, 89
      hot site agreement, 86–87
      plan development, 86, 90
      plan evaluation, 86, 90–91
      plan testing, 86, 90
      software backup, 87–88
      strategy options, 86–87
      telecommunications backup, 89–90
   computer operations, 67–73
      duty separation/rotation, 68–69
      equipment control, 70
      equipment maintenance, 69–70
      library control, 71–72
      operator control, 71

Information systems *(continued)*
      transaction processing, 72–73
      workload scheduling, 70
   data integrity
      computer virus control, 84–85
      output control, 81–82
      telecommunication control, 82
      transmission control, 83–84
      user education, 85
   development/programming, 60–67
      database administrator, 67
      database monitoring, 67
      data security, 66–67
      development standards, 61–62
      manual documentation, 66
      program documentation, 61, 65–66
      programming personnel, 64–65
      program modification, 64
      program security, 65
      program testing, 63
      project control, 61
      software implementation, 63
      software selection, 62
      system development life cycle (SDLC), 62
   document imaging, 106
   electronic funds transfer (EFT)
      automated clearing house (ACH), 96
      automated teller machines (ATMs), 94
      communication control, 94
      credit risk, 92–93
      insurance for, 100–101
      internal control, 98–101
      internet banking, 97–98
      nondeposit investment products, 98
      operational control, 93
      payment order origination, 91–92
      PINs, 95, 98–100
      point–of–sale (POS), 94–95
      retail, 94, 98–101
      risk control, 92
      smart cards, 95
      wholesale, 91
   end–user computing (EUC)
      acquisition criteria, 102
      communications in, 105–6
      development of, 103–4
      existing inventory, 101–2
      security for, 102–3
      usage of, 104–5
   external audits, 57
   internal audits
      application development/testing, 56–57
      auditor role, 55–56
      frequency of, 56
      independent, 55
      scope of, 56
   management of
      insurance coverage, 59–60
      internal control, 58–59

Information systems *(continued)*
    organization, 57–58
    outsourcing arrangements, 60
    planning, 58
    policies/procedures, 58
    reports, 59
    technology, 60
  overview of, 54
  references regarding, 107
  security
    administration of, 74–75
    building protection, 76
    computer protection, 76–77
    contingency planning, 76
    data protection, 77–78
    logical access control, 78–79
    network protection, 76–77
    plan for, 75–76
    principles of, 73–74
    provisions of, 74
    system logs, 79–81
    unauthorized disclosures, 81
Insurance. *See specific insurances*
Interagency Guidelines Establishing Standards for Safety and Soundness (1995)
  agency authority, 195
  compliance plan requirement, 195–96
  enforcement of, 196
  operational standards, 194–95
Interest rate risk, 15
Internet banking, 97–98
Interstate Act (1994), 9–10

L

Legal risk, 15, 18
Library control
  private library, 71–72
  production library, 71
  test library, 71
Licensing, 8
  dual system of, 11
  revocations
    conservatorship and, 186
    foreign banks, 186–87
    receivership and, 185–86
Line grabbing, 83–84
Liquidity
  rating systems and, 128, 133–34
  risk in, 15, 18
Logs, 79–81

M

Market risk, 15, 18
Masquerading, 83

N

National Automated Clearing House Association (NACHA), 96
National banks, 6, 11

National Bank Surveillance System (NBSS), 122, 174–75
National Credit Union Administration (NCUA), 7
Network protection, 76–77
Non–depository institutions, 7

O

Office of the Comptroller of the Currency (OCC)
  rating systems and, 125, 146, 175
  regulatory enforcement and, 185–87
  regulatory examination and, 48
  regulatory system and, 11
  risk–focused examination and, 14–15, 16
Office of Thrift Supervision (OTS)
  rating systems and, 125–26
  regulatory examination and, 48
  risk–focused examination and, 17–18
Operational risk, 15, 17
Opting–out, 9–10
Outsourcing
  information systems, 60
  internal audits, 30–31

P

Penalties
  civil money
    in general, 182–83
    for holding companies, 183–84
    reports and, 183
  sentencing guidelines and, 191
Personnel
  compliance function and, 42–43
  information systems and
    application programmers, 64–65
    system programmers, 65
  regulatory examination and, 51
Piggybacking, 83
PINs, 95, 98–100
Point–of–sale (POS) transaction, 94–95
Power limitations, 8
Price risk, 15
Private library, 71–72
Production library, 71

Q

Qualified report, 34–35

R

Ratings systems
  BOPEC
    bank condition, 156–57
    capital adequacy, 162–65
    consolidated earnings, 160–62
    finances, 154
    management, 154–56
    nonbank condition, 157–59

Index 201

Ratings systems *(continued)*
    overview of, 122, 151–54
    parent company, 159–60
    risk management, 165–67
  Community Reinvestment performance, 122
  Consumer Compliance
    composite ratings, 168–70
    FDIC and, 170
    overview of, 122, 167–68
  five–point scale for, 122–25
  foreign banks
    annual examination plan, 150–51
    Combined rating, 148
    ROCA, 122, 146–48, 150
    SOSA, 122, 149–50
  off–site
    NBSS, 122, 174–75
    SEER, 122, 174–75
  Uniform Financial Institutions Rating System (UFIRS) (CAMELS), 122, 125–37
    asset quality, 128, 129–30
    CAMELS acronym, 128
    capital adequacy, 128, 129
    earnings, 128, 132–33
    FDICIA connection, 136–37
    liquidity, 128, 133–34
    management/administration, 128, 130–32
    market risk sensitivity, 128, 134–36
    overview of, 125–27
    performance evaluation, 128–36
  Uniform Interagency/Data Processing Organizations, 122, 170–74
    audits, 171
    computer operations, 174
    management, 172–73
    systems/programming, 173
  Uniform Interagency Trust Rating System (UITRS), 122, 137–46
    account administration, 141–42
    asset administration, 140–41
    conflict of interest, 142–43
    earnings/volume trends/prospects, 143–45
    operations/controls/audits, 139–40
    proposed changes for, 145–46
    supervision/organization, 138–39
Records
  compliance function and
    establishment of, 43
    review of, 43–44
  regulatory examination and, 51
Regulatory enforcement
  formal, 178–84
    cease–and–desist orders, 179–80
    cease–and–desist orders, temporary, 180
    civil money penalty, 182–83
    civil money penalty/holding companies, 183–84
    civil money penalty/reports, 183
    institution–affiliated party removal, 180–82
    insurance termination, 184

Regulatory enforcement *(continued)*
  informal, 178
  license revocations
    conservatorship, 186
    foreign bank office termination, 186–87
    receivership, 185–86
  overview of, 178
Regulatory examination
  management of
    documentation, 50
    examination coordinator, 50–51
    examiner treatment, 52
    First Day Letter, 49
    information control, 51
    personnel training, 51
    policy awareness, 52
    prior exception corrections, 52
  objectives of, 48–49
  procedures for, 49
  process of, 48
  records for, 51
  reports for, 48–49
  See also Risk–focused examination
Regulatory system
  bank holding companies, 9
    geographic restrictions, 10
    securities activities, 10–11
  commercial banks, 6
    geographic restrictions, 9–10
  credit unions, 7
  deposit insurance, 6, 7, 8, 11–12
  federal/state regulations, 11–12
    dual system of, 11
  geographic restrictions
    bank holding companies, 10
    commercial banks, 9–10
    de novo branches, 10
    Interstate Act (1994), 9–10
    opting–out, 9–10
    savings associations, 10
  licensing/approval, 8
  national banks, 6, 11
  non–depository institutions, 7
  power limitations, 8
  reserve requirements, 8–9
  savings associations, 7
    geographic restrictions, 10
    savings and loan holding company, 9
    unitary savings and loan holding company, 9
  securities activities, 10–11
  state banks, 6, 11
  supervisory oversight, 8
Report of Condition and Income (Call Report), 183
Reports
  external audits
    adverse, 35
    disclaimer, 35
    qualified, 34–35
    standards for, 33

Reports *(continued)*
   unqualified, 34
   information systems, 59
   internal audits, 29
   regulatory examination, 48–49
Reputation risk, 15
Reserve requirements, 8–9
Riegle–Neal Interstate Banking and Branching Efficiency Act (1994), 9–10
Risk–focused examination
   agency differences in, 14–15
      risk categories, 15
   audits and, 18–19, 20
   compliance risk, 15, 18–19
   credit risk, 15, 17, 19, 20
   FDIC and, 16–17
   Federal Reserve System and, 14–15
   foreign exchange risk, 15
   FRB and, 16
   interest rate risk, 15
   legal risk, 15, 18
   liquidity risk, 15, 18
   market risk, 15, 18
   OCC and, 14–15, 16
   operational risk, 15, 17
   OTS and, 17–18
   price risk, 15
   process of, 16
   renewed emphasis on, 14
   reputation risk, 15
   risk management in, 19–20
   strategic risk, 15, 18
   transaction risk, 15
ROCA rating system, 122, 146–48, 150

S

Savings and Loan Holding Company Act, 184
Savings Association Insurance Fund (SAIF), 7
Savings associations, 7
   geographic restrictions, 10
   savings and loan holding company, 9
   unitary savings and loan holding company, 9
Securities activities, 10–11
Sentencing guidelines
   compliance program and
      effective elements of, 190–91
      importance of, 190
   internal reporting systems, 192
   penalty range, 191
   purpose of, 190
   voluntary disclosure and, 191–92
Smart cards, 95
Software
   backup for, 87–88
   implementation of, 63
   selection of, 62
SOSA rating system, 122, 149–50

Standards
   external audits, 32–33
      fieldwork, 33
      general, 33
      reports, 33
      generally accepted auditing standards (GAAS), 32–33, 34–35
   information systems, 61–62
   risk–based audits, 24–25
   See also Interagency Guidelines Establishing Standards for Safety and Soundness (1995)
State banks, 6, 11
State regulations, 11–12
Strategic risk, 15, 18
Supervision by risk. *See* Risk–focused examination
Supervisory oversight, 8
SWIFT, 91
Systems to Estimate Examination Ratings (SEER), 122, 174–75

T

Technology, 7, 60
Telecommunications, 7
   in business recovery planning (BRP), 89–90
   data integrity and, 82
Test library, 71
Transaction risk, 15
   audits and, 22
   information systems and, 54

U

Uniform Bank Surveillance Screen (UBSS), 175
Uniform Commercial Code Article 4A (UCC4A), 91–92
Uniform Financial Institutions Rating System (UFIRS) (CAMELS), 122, 125–37
   asset quality, 128, 129–30
   CAMELS acronym, 128
   capital adequacy, 128, 129
   earnings, 128, 132–33
   FDICIA connection, 136–37
   liquidity, 128, 133–34
   management/administration, 128, 130–32
   market risk sensitivity, 128, 134–36
   overview of, 125–27
   performance evaluation, 128–36
Uniform Interagency Rating System/Data Processing Organizations, 122, 170–74
   audits, 171
   computer operations, 174
   management, 172–73
   systems/programming, 173
Uniform Interagency Trust Rating System (UITRS), 122, 137–46
   account administration, 141–42
   asset administration, 140–41
   conflict of interest, 142–43

Uniform Interagency Trust Rating System (UITRS) *(continued)*
    earnings/volume trends/prospects, 143–45
    operations/controls/audits, 139–40
    proposed changes for, 145–46
    supervision/organization, 138–39
Unqualified report, 34

Y

Year 2000 problem
    board of director responsibility, 112–13
    certification requirements, 116–18
    consumer issues, 111
    external risks, 111
        corporate customers, 118
        data exchange, 118

Year 2000 problem *(continued)*
        vendor relations, 118
    foreign banks and, 111
    industry coordination, 118
    operational issues
        contracts, 119
        mergers/acquisitions, 119
        replacement vs. repair, 119
        special dates, 119
    overview of, 110
    project assessment, 114
    project guidelines, 115–16
    project on–site examination, 114–15
    project planning, 113–14
    supervisory follow–up for, 111–12
    Y2K timeline for, 110, 117–18